Relational Database Design Clearly Explained

Jan L. Harrington

AP PROFESSIONAL

AP PROFESSIONAL is a division of Academic Press

San Diego   London   Boston
New York   Sydney   Tokyo   Toronto

Copyright © 1998 by Academic Press
All rights reserved.

AP Professional
1300 Boylston Street, Chestnut Hill, MA 02167, USA
An Imprint of Academic Press
A Division of Harcourt Brace & Company
http://www.apnet.com

ACADEMIC PRESS
24–28 Oval Road, London NW1 7DX
http://www.hbuk.co.uk/ao/

Library of Congress Cataloging-in-Publication Data
Harrington, Jan L.
    Relational Database Design Clearly Explained / Jan L. Harrington
        p.   cm.
    Includes index.
    ISBN 0-12-326425-1
    1. Relational databases.   2. Database design   I. Title
QA76.9.D26H38   1998
005.75'65—dc21
                                                                98-8472
                                                                CIP

Printed in the United States of America
98 99 00 01 02 CP 9 8 7 6 5 4 3 2 1

Contents

Chapter 4: Normalization 63

Chapter 5: Database Structure and Performance Tuning 89

Chapter 6: Codd's Rules 97

Part Two: Practice   109

Chapter 7: Using SQL to Implement a Relational Design   111

Preface

My favorite opening line for the database courses I teach is: "Probably the most misunderstood term in all of business computing is *database*, followed closely by the word *relational*." At that point, the students often snicker, because they are absolutely, positively sure that they know what a database is and that they also know what it means for a database to be relational. Unfortunately, the popular press has distorted the meaning of both those terms and led to many businesses thinking that designing a database is a task that can be left to a clerical worker who has taken a few days training in using database software. As you will see throughout this book, nothing could be further from the truth.

> *Note: By the same token, I have received applications for adjunct faculty positions from people who say they know how to use Microsoft Access or Paradox or FileMaker Pro and therefore believe they are qualified to teach a database theory course. From where I sit, that is pretty scary.*

I have wanted to write a book like this for a long time. We teach relation database design theory to college students, but it is a rare pleasure to get the chance to share that theory—and the practice of that theory—with the business community, with people who are actually doing such designs in their jobs.

This book is intended for anyone who has been given the responsibility of designing or maintaining a relational database. The first part will teach you how to look at the environment your database serves and to tailor the design of that database to the environment. It will also teach you ways of designing the database so that it provides accurate and consistent data, avoiding the problems that are common to poorly designed databases. In addition, you will read about design compromises that you might choose to make in the interest of database application performance and the consequences of making such choices.

Part II looks at the more practical aspects of performing database design, covering the implementation of a design using SQL and using a CASE tool to help document and support the design process. In addition, Part II contains three large database design case studies, each of which presents one or more design challenges that you may encounter when designing relational databases.

What You Need to Know

Because this book deals primarily with database design, you do not need any special computing background to read it. You should, however, have some basic computer literacy. If you know how to get around your computer's operating system, run programs someone has written for you, then you know enough to understand the material in Part I and most of Part II of this book. To get the most out of Chapter 8 (using SQL to implement a relational design), you should be familiar with some type of database environment that provides an interface for sending SQL commands to a database.

Acknowledgments

Writing a book for the folks at AP Professional is always a joy. I would therefore like to thank the following individuals who helped make this one possible:

- Ken Morton, Editor, who, as always, is an immense pleasure to work with.
- Thomas Park, Assistant Editor, who provided support whenever it was needed.
- Jennifer Vilaga, Editorial Assistant, who looks after all the details.
- Bettina Burch, Production Editor, who made getting this book into print very, very simple.
- Mary Prescott, the copy editor, who has a great eye and a light hand.
- Robert Standefer, the reviewer, who added his very welcome expertise.
- Carole McClendon, my agent, who hooked me up with AP Professional in the first place.

JLH

Part One

Theory

The first part of this book considers the theoretical aspects of relational database design. You will read about identifying data relationships in your database environment, the details of the relational data model, and how to translate data relationships into a well-designed relational database that avoids most of the problems associated with bad designs.

1

Introduction

So many of today's businesses rely on their database systems for accurate, up-to-date information. Without those repositories of mission-critical data, most businesses are unable to perform their normal daily transactions, much less create summary reports that help management make strategic corporate decisions. To be useful, the data in a database must be accurate, complete, and organized in such a way that data can be retrieved when needed and in the format required.

Well-written database application programs are fundamental to timely and accurate data retrieval. However, without a good underlying database design, even the best program cannot avoid problems with inaccurate and inconsistent data. That is what this book is all about: to help you learn to design good relational databases that avoid many of the problems inherent in poor database design.

Good database design means that you take time to plan your database before you put it into use. It means that you focus on the way your business works and tailor that database to your own organization's specifications. What do you get for all this work? You get a database that accurately supports the needs of your company, that provides everyone who uses it with accurate, complete information.

Effects of Poor Database Design

To make it a bit clearer why the design of a database matters so much, let us take a look at a business that has a very bad design, and the problems that the poor design brings. The business is named Lasers Only.

> Note: We will leave the precise definition of a database for later. As you will see, the data storage used by Lasers Only is not precisely a database.

Back in the early 1980s, when most people were just discovering video tapes, Mark Watkins and Emily Stone stumbled across a fledgling technology known as the laser disc. There were several competing formats, but by 1986 the industry had standardized on a 12-inch silver platter on which either 30 or 60 minutes of video and audio could be recorded. Although the market was still small, it was at that time that Watkins and Smith opened Lasers Only, a business that sold and rented laser discs.

Today, Lasers Only carries laser discs, audio CDs, and DVDs. (There is still great disagreement between videophiles as to whether the DVDs are better than the 12-inch laser discs.) The company rents titles from its single retail store. However, the largest part of its business comes from sales, both in the store and through mail order.

In 1990, when the store began its mail order business, Watkins created a "database" to handle the orders and sales. Customers were (and still are) enticed to order titles before the official release date by offering a 15 to 20 percent discount on preorders. (All titles are always discounted 10 percent from the suggested retail price.) The mail order database therefore needed to include a way to handle backorders so that preordered items could be shipped as soon as they came into the store.

At the time we visit Lasers Only, they are still using the software Watkins created. The primary data entry interface is a form like that in Figure 1-1. Each time a customer orders a single title, an employee of the store fills out the entire form.

Figure 1-1: The data entry form used by Lasers Only for their mail order business

Customer numbers are created by combining the customer's zip code, the first three letters of his or her last name, and a three-digit sequence number. For example, if Stone lives in zip code 12345 and she is the second customer in that zip code with a last name beginning with STO, then her customer number is 12345STO002. The sequence number ensures that no two customer numbers will be alike.

When a new title comes into the store, an employee searches the database to find all people who have ordered that title. The employee prints a packing slip from the stored data and then places an X in the Item shipped? check box.

At first glance, the Lasers Only software seems pretty simple and straightforward. Should work just fine, right? Well, it worked for a while, but after a year or two, serious problems began to arise.

Unnecessary Duplicated Data and Data Consistency

The Lasers Only database has a considerable amount of unnecessary duplicated data:

- A customer's name, address, and phone number are duplicated for every item the customer orders.
- A merchandise item's title is duplicated every time the item is ordered.

What is the problem with this duplication? When you have duplicated data in this way, the data should be the same throughout the database. In other words, every order for a given customer should have the same name, address, and phone number, typed exactly the same way. Every order for a single title should have the same title, typed exactly the same way. We want the duplicated data to be consistent throughout the database.

As the database grows larger, this type of consistency is very hard to maintain. Most business-oriented database software is *case sensitive*, in that it considers upper- and lowercase letters to be different characters. In addition, no one is a perfect typist. A difference in capitalization or even a single mistyped letter will cause database software to consider two values to be distinct.

When a Lasers Only employee performs a search to find all people who have ordered a specific title, the database software will retrieve only those orders that match the title entered by the employee exactly. For example, assume that a movie named Summer Days is scheduled to be released soon. In some orders, the title is stored correctly as "Summer Days." However, in others it is stored as "summer days" or even "Sumer Days." When an employee searches for all the people to whom the movie should be shipped, the orders for "summer days" and "Sumer Days" will not be retrieved. Those customers will not receive their orders, causing disgruntled customers and probably lost business.

The current Lasers Only software has no way to ensure that duplicated data are entered consistently. There are two solutions. The first is to eliminate as much of the duplicated data as possible. (As you will see, it is neither possible nor desireable to eliminate all of it.) The second is to provide some mechanism for verifying that when data must be duplicated, they are entered correctly. A well-designed database will do both.

> Note: Unnecessary duplicated data also take up extra disk space, but given that disk space is relatively inexpensive today, that is not a major reason for getting rid of the redundant data.

Data Insertion Problems

Lasers Only prepares its catalog of forthcoming titles by hand. Each month when the announcements of new releases arrive from the distributors, an employee does a manual "cut and paste" operation to assemble a 16-page booklet that can be duplicated and mailed to customers. In 1995, however, Stone realized that this was a very cumbersome process and thought it would be much better if the catalog could be generated from the database.

Why not get a list of forthcoming titles from the database and have a database program generate the entire catalog? As she discovered, it could not be done. There are two major reasons.

First, the current database does not contain all the information needed for the catalog, in particular a synopsis of the content of the disc. This problem could be remedied by adding that information to the current database. However, doing so would only exacerbate the problem with unnecessary duplicated data if the company were to include the summary with every order. If the summary were to be included only once, how would the company know which order contained the summary?

Second, and by far more important, there is no way to enter data about a title unless someone has ordered it. This presents a rather large Catch-22. Lasers Only cannot insert data about a title until it has been ordered at least once, but no one can receive a computer-generated catalog knowing that it is available to be ordered unless someone can get the data into the database.

> Note: This problem is more formally known as an "insertion anomaly," and you will learn about it more formally throughout this book.

Data Deletion Problems

Lasers Only also has problems when it comes to deleting data. Assume, for example, that a customer orders only one item. After the order has been processed, the item is discontinued by the manufacturer. Lasers Only therefore wants to delete all references to the item from its database because the item is no longer available.

When the orders containing the item are deleted, information about any customer who has ordered only that item is also deleted. No other orders remain in the database for that customer. Lasers Only will be unable to send that customer any more catalogs and therefore loses the chance of getting any more business from that customer.

> Note: This problem is more formally known as a "deletion anomaly." It, too, will be discussed in greater depth throughout this book.

Meaningful Identifiers

The Lasers Only database has another major problem: those customer numbers. It is very tempting to code meaning into identifiers and it usually works well — until the values on which the idenifiers are based change.

Consider what happens when a Lasers Only customer moves. The person's customer number must change. At that point, there will be orders for the same customer with two different customer numbers in the same database.

If a customer who has moved since first ordering from the store calls and asks for a list of all items he or she has on order, the first thing the employee who answers the telephone does is ask the customer for his or her customer number. The customer, of course, provides the current value, which means that anything ordered under the old customer number will be missed during a search. The customer may assume that titles ordered under the old customer number are not on order. As a result, the customer may place another order, causing two copies of the same item to be shipped. Lasers Only is then faced with another disgruntled customer who has to make the effort to send back the duplicate and get the second charge removed from his or her credit card.

What You Will Find in This Book

The purpose of this book is to help you avoid the types of problems about which you have just read. A well-designed database provides ways to eliminate much data redundancy, enforce data consistency, allow data entry as needed without requiring you to enter "extra" data, and allow data deletion without accidentally losing data you want to keep.

In Chapter 2 we begin by looking at the foundation of database design: identifying logical data relationships in the environment the database will serve, without reference to the software you will be using. Then, in Chapter 3, we turn to data models, the formal way in which you express data relationships to database software. There you will meet the relational data model for the first time and begin to understand what it means for a database to be relational. In Chapters 4 through 7, we'll explore the details of the relational data model, and finish with Chapter 8, in which you will learn how to use SQL (the standard language for interacting with relational databases) to create the relational database elements about which you have been reading. Along the way we will redesign and expand the Lasers Only database to give the company a workable design on which to build database applications.

In Chapter 9 you will be introduced to the role of software tools that support database design activities. Chapters 10 through 12 contain database design case studies that present a variety of database design challenges that you may encounter.

2

Entities and Data Relationships

In this chapter we will explore the fundamental concept behind all databases: There are things in a business environment about which we need to store data and those things are related to one another in a variety of ways. In fact, to be considered a *database*, the place where data are stored must contain not only the data but also information about the relationships between those data.

The idea behind a database is that the user—either a person working interactively or an application program—has no need to worry about the way in which data are physically stored on disk. The user phrases data manipulation requests in terms of data relationships. A piece of software known as a *database management system* (DBMS) then translates between the user's request for data and the physical data storage.

The formal way in which you express data relationships to a DBMS is known as a *data model*. The relational data model, about which you will learn in this book, is just such a formal structure. However, the underlying relationships in a database environment are independent of the data model and therefore also independent of the DBMS you are using. Before you can design a database for any data model, you need to be able to identify data relationships.

> *Note: Most DBMSs support only one data model. Therefore, when you choose a DBMS, you are also choosing your data model.*

In this chapter we will explore data relationships and their characteristics. You will also learn a DBMS-independent technique for documenting those relationships known as the *entity–relationship diagram* (ER diagram).

Entities and Their Attributes

An *entity* is something about which we store data. A customer is an entity, as is a merchandise item stocked by Lasers Only. Entities are not necessarily tangible. For example, an event such as a concert is an entity; an appointment to see the doctor is an entity.

Entities have data that describe them (their *attributes*). For example, a customer entity is usually described by a customer number, first name, last name, street, city, state, zip, and phone number. A concert entity might be described by a title, date, location, and name of the performer.

When we represent entities in a database, we actually store only the attributes. Each group of attributes that describes a single real-world occurrence of an entity acts to represent an *instance* of an entity. For example, in Figure 2-1, you can see four instances of a customer entity stored in a database. If we have 1000 customers in our database, then there will be 1000 collections of customer attributes.

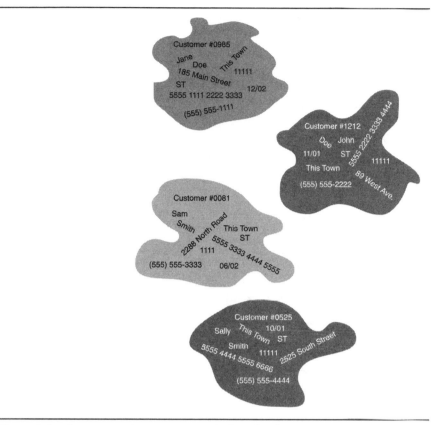

Figure 2-1:   Instances of a customer entiy in a database

Note: Keep in mind that we are not making any statements about how the instances are physically stored. What you see in Figure 2-1 is purely a conceptual representation.

Entity Identifiers

The only purpose for putting the data that describe an entity into a database is to retrieve the data at some later date. This means that we must have some way of distinguishing one entity from another so that we can always be certain that we are retrieving the precise entity we want. We do this by ensuring that each entity has some attribute values that distinguish it from every other entity in the database (an *entity identifier*).

Assume, for example, that Lasers Only has two customers named John Smith. If an employee searches for the items John Smith has on order, which John Smith will the DMBS retrieve? In this case, both of them. Because there is no way to distinguish between the two customers, the result of the query will be inaccurate.

Lasers Only solved the problem by creating unique customer numbers. That is indeed a common solution to identifying instances of entities where there is no simple unique identifier suggested by the data themselves.

Another solution would be to pair the customer's first and last names with his or her telephone number. This combination of columns (a *concatenated identifier*) would also uniquely identify each customer. There are, however, two drawbacks to doing so. First, the identifier is long and clumsy; it would be easy to make mistakes when entering any of the parts. Second, if the customer's phone number changes, then the identifier must also change. As you read in Chapter 1, changes in an entity identifier can cause serious problems in a database.

Some entities, such as invoices, come with natural identifiers (the invoice number). We give unique, meaningless numbers to others — especially people, places, and things. Still others require concatenated identifiers.

> Note: We will examine the issue of what makes a good unique identifier more closely in Chapter 3, when we talk about "primary keys."

When we store an instance of an entity in a database, we want the DBMS to ensure that the new instance has a unique identifier. This is an example of a *constraint* on a database, a rule to which data must adhere. The enforcement of a variety of database constraints helps us to maintain data consistency and accuracy.

Single-Valued Versus Multivalued Attributes

Because we are eventually going to create a relational database, the attributes in our data model must be *single-valued*. This means that for a given instance of an entity, each attribute can have only one value. For example, a customer entity allows only one telephone number for each customer. If a customer has more than one phone number and wants them all included in the database, then the customer entity cannot handle them.

> Note: While it is true that the entity–relationship model of a database is independent of the formal data model used to express the structure of the data to a DBMS, we often make decisions on how to model the data based on the requirements of the formal data model we will be using. Removing multivalued attributes is one such case. You will also see an example of this when we deal with many-to-many relationships between entities.

The existence of more than one phone number turns the phone number attribute into a *multivalued attribute*. Because an entity in a relational database cannot have multivalued attributes, you must handle those attributes by creating an entity to hold them.

In the case of the multiple phone numbers, we could create a phone number entity. Each instance of the entity would include the customer number of the person to whom the phone number belonged along with the telephone number. If a customer had three phone numbers, then there would be three instances of the phone number entity for the customer. The entity's identifier would be the concatenation of the customer number and the telephone number.

> Note: There is no way to avoid using the telephone number as part of the entity identifier in the telephone number entity. As you will come to understand as you read this book, in this particular case there is no harm in using it in this way.

As a general rule, if you run across a multivalued attribute, this is a major hint that you need another attribute. The only way to handle multiple values of the same attribute is to create an entity of which you can store multiple instances, once for each value of the attribute.

Avoiding Collections of Entities

When you first begin to work with entities, the nature of an entity can be somewhat confusing. Consider, for example, the merchandise inventory handled by Lasers Only. Is "inventory" an entity? No. Inventory is a collection of the merchandise items handled by the store. The entity is actually the merchandise item. Viewing all of the instances of the merchandise item entity as a whole provides the inventory.

To make this a bit clearer, consider the attributes you would need if you decided to include an inventory entity: merchandise item number, item title, number in stock, retail price, and so on. But because you are trying to describe an entire inventory with a single entity, you need multiple values for each of those attributes. As you read earlier, however, attributes cannot be multivalued. This tells you that inventory cannot stand as an entity. It must be represented as a collection of instances of a merchandise item entity.

As another example, consider a person's medical history maintained by a doctor. Like an inventory, a medical history is a collection of more than one entity. A medical history is made up of appointments and the events that occur during those appointments. Therefore, the history is really a collection of instances of appointment entities and medical treatment entities. The "history" is an output that a database application can obtain by gathering the data stored in the underlying entity instances.

Documenting Entities and Attributes

Entity-relationship diagrams provide a way to document the entities in a database along with the attributes that describe them. There are actually several styles of ER diagrams. The two most commonly used styles are Chen (named after the originator of ER modeling) and Information Engineering. It does not matter which you use, as long as everyone who is using the diagram understands its symbols.

Both the Chen and Information Engineering models use rectangles to represent entities. Each entity's name appears in the rectangle and is expressed in the singular, as in

customer

The original Chen model has no provision for showing attributes on the ER diagram itself. However, many people have extended the model to include the attributes in ovals:

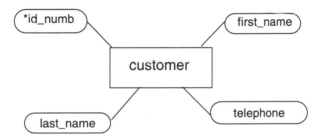

The entity's identifier is the attribute preceded by an asterisk (*id_numb).

The Information Engineering model includes the attributes in the rectangle with the entity:

customer

*id_numb
first_name
last_name
telephone

Because the Information Engineering model tends to produce a less cluttered diagram, we will be using it for most of diagrams in this book, although you will be introduced to elements of both models throughout this chapter.

Entities and Attributes for Lasers Only

The major entities and their attributes for the Lasers Only database can be found in Figure 2-2. As you will see, the design will require additional entities as we work with the relationships between those already identified. In particular, there is no information in Figure 2-2 that indicates which items appear on which orders because that information is a part of the logical relationship between orders and items.

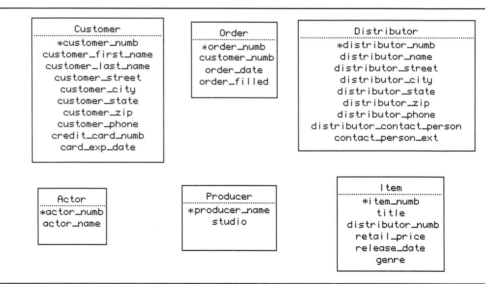

Figure 2-2: Major entities and their attributes for the Lasers Only database

The entities in Figure 2-2 and the remainder of the ER diagrams in this book were created with a special type of software known as a *CASE tool* (computer-aided software engineering). CASE tools provide a wide range of data and systems modeling assistance. You will find more detail on how CASE tools support the database design process in Chapter 9.

Note: The specific product used for these diagrams was MacA&D, which provides capabilities typical of most professional CASE tools.

Domains

Each attribute has a *domain*, an expression of the permissible values for that attribute. A domain can be very small. For example, a T-shirt store might have a Size attribute for its merchandise items with the values L, XL, and XXL comprising the entire domain. In contrast, an attribute for a customer's first name is very large and might be specified only as "text" or "human names."

A DBMS enforces a domain through a *domain constraint*. Whenever a value is stored in the database, the DBMS verifies that it comes from its attribute's specified domain. Although in many cases we cannot specify small domains, at the very least the domain assures us that we are getting data of the right type. For example, a DBMS can prevent a user from storing 123x50 in an attribute whose domain is currency values. Most DBMSs also provide fairly tight domain checking on date and time attributes, which can help you avoid dates such as February 30.

Documenting Domains

The common formats used for ER diagrams do not usually include domains on the diagrams themselves, but store the domains in an associated document (usually a *data dictionary*, something about which you will read much more throughout this book). However, the version of the Chen method that includes attributes can also include domains by placing an expression of the domain underneath each attribute. Notice in Figure 2-3 that three of the domains are fairly general (integer and character), while the domain for the telephone number attribute includes a very specific format. Whether a domain can be constrained in this way depends on the DBMS .

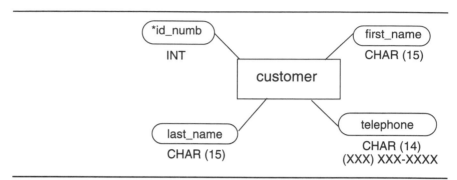

Figure 2-3:   Indicating domains on an ER diagram

Practical Domain Choices

The domains that Lasers Only chooses for its attributes should theoretically be independent of the DBMS that the company will use. In practical terms, however, it makes little sense to assign domains that you cannot implement. Therefore, the database designer working for Lasers Only takes a look at the DBMS to see what column data types are supported.

Most relational DBMSs that use SQL as their query language provide the following among their column data types, any of which can be assigned as a domain to an attribute:

- ◆ CHAR: A fixed-length string of text, usually up to 256 characters.
- ◆ VARCHAR: A variable-length string of text, usually up to 256 characters.
- ◆ INT: An integer, the size of which varies depending on the operation system.
- ◆ DECIMAL and NUMERIC: Real numbers, with fractional portions to the right of the decimal point. When you assign a real number domain, you must specifiy how many digits the number can contain (including the decimal point) and how many digits should be to the right of the decimal point (the value's *precision*). For example, currency values usually have precision of two,

so a number in the format XXX.XX might have a domain of DECIMAL (6,2).
- DATE: A date.
- TIME: A time.
- DATETIME: The combination of a date and a time.
- BOOLEAN: A logical value (either true or false).

Many of today's DBMSs also support a data type known as a BLOB (binary large object) that can store anything binary, such as a graphic.

Choosing the right domain can make a big difference in the accuracy of a database. For example, a U.S. zip code is made up of five or nine digits. Should an attribute for a zip code therefore be given a domain of INT? No, for two reasons. First, it would be nice to be able to include the hyphen in nine-digit zip codes. Second, and more important, zip codes in the northeast begin with a zero. If they are stored as a number, the leading zero disappears. Therefore, we always choose a CHAR domain for zip codes. Since we never do arithmetic with zip codes, nothing is lost by using character rather than numeric storage.

By the same token, it is important to choose domains of DATE and TIME for chronological data. As an example, consider what would happen if the dates 01/12/2000 and 08/12/1999 were stored as characters. If you ask the DBMS to choose which date comes first, the DBMS will compare the character strings in alphabetical order, and respond that 01/12/2000 comes first, because 01 alphabetically precedes 08. The only way to get character dates to order correctly is to use the format YYYY/MM/DD, a format that is rarely used anywhere in the world. However, if the dates were given a domain of DATE, then the DBMS would order them properly. The DBMS would also be able to perform date arithmetic, finding the interval between two dates or adding constants (for example, 30 days) to dates.

Basic Data Relationships

Once you have a good idea of the basic entities in your database environment, your next task is to identify the relationships among those entities. There are three basic types of relationships that you may encounter: one-to-one, one-to-many, and many-to-many.

Before turning to the types of relationships themselves, there is one important thing to keep in mind: The relationships that are stored in a database are between instances of entities. For example, a Lasers Only customer is related to the items he or she orders. Each instance of the customer entity is related to instances of the specific items ordered (see Figure 2-4).

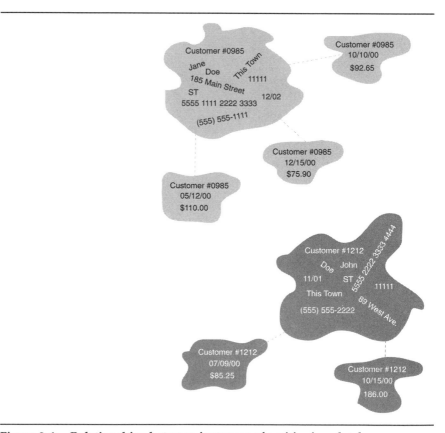

Figure 2-4:   Relationships between instances of entities in a database

> *Note: As you look at Figure 2-4, once again remember that this
> is a purely conceptual representation of what is in the database
> and is completely unrelated to the physical storage of the data.*

When we document data relationships, such as when we draw an
ER diagram, we show the types of relationships among entities. We
are showing the possible relationships that are allowable in the database. Unless we specify that a relationship is mandatory, there is
no requirement that every instance of every entity be involved in
every documented relationship. For example, Lasers Only could
store data about a customer without the customer having any current orders to which it is related.

One-to-One Relationships

Consider, for a moment, an airport in a small town and the town in
which the airport is located, both of which are described in a database of small town airports. Each of these might be represented as
an instance of a different type of entity. The relationships between
the two instances can then be expressed as "The airport is located in
one and only one town and the town contains one and only one airport."

This is a true *one-to-one relationship* because at no time can a single
airport be related to more than one town and no town can be related
to more than one airport. (Although there are municipalities that
have more than one airport, the towns in this database are too small
for that to ever happen.)

Another true one-to-one relationship is that of the traditional mar-
riage. A man can be married to no woman or one woman; a woman
can be married to no man or one man.

If we have two instances of two entities (A and B) called A_i and B_i,
then a one-to-one relationship exists if at all times A_i is related to no
instances of entity B or one instance of entity B, and B_i is related to
no instances of entity A or one instance of entity A.

True one-to-one relationships are very rare in business. For example, assume that Lasers Only decides to start dealing with a new distributor of laser discs. At first, the company orders only one specialty title from the new distributor. If we peered inside the database, we would see that the instance of the distributor entity was related to just the one merchandise item instance. This would then appear to be a one-to-one relationship. However, over time Lasers Only may choose to order more titles from the new distributor, which would violate the rule that the distributor must be related to no more than one merchandise item. What we have is therefore not a true one-to-one relationship. (This is an example of a one-to-many relationship, which is discussed in the next section of this chapter.)

By the same token, what if Lasers Only created a special credit card entity to hold data about the credit cards that renters used to secure their rentals? Each customer has only one credit card on file with the store. There would therefore seem to be a one-to-one relationship between the instance of a customer entity and the instance of the credit card entity. However, in this case we are really dealing with a single entity. The credit card number, the type of credit card, and the credit card's expiration date can all become attributes of the customer entity. Given that only one credit card is stored for each customer, the attributes are not multivalued; no separate entity is needed.

If you think you are dealing with a one-to-one relationship, look at it very carefully. Be sure that you are not really looking at a one-to-many relationship or that what you think is two entities should really be one.

One-to-Many Relationships

The most common type of relationship is a *many-to-many relationship*. (In fact, most relational databases are comprised of only one-to-many relationships.) For example, Lasers Only typically orders many titles from each distributor and a given title comes from only one distributor. By the same token, a customer places many orders but an order comes from only one customer.

If we have instances of two entities (A and B), then a one-to-many relationship exists between two instances (A_i and B_i) if A_i is related to zero, one, or more instances of entity B and B_i is related to zero or one instance of entity A.

Other many-to-many relationships include that between a child and her biological mother. A woman may have zero, one, or more biological daughters; a daughter has only one biological mother. As another example, consider a computer and its CPU. A CPU may not be installed in any computer or it may be installed in at most one computer; a computer may have no CPU, one CPU, or more than one CPU.

The example of Lasers Only and the distributor from which the company ordered only one title is actually a one-to-many relationship where the "many" is currently "one." Remember that when we are specifying data relationships, we are indicating possible relationships and not necessarily requiring that all instances of all entities participate in every documented relationship. There is absolutely no requirement that a distributor be related to any merchandise item, much less one or more merchandise items. (It might not make much sense to have a distributor in the database from whom the company did not order, but there is nothing to prevent data about that distributor from being stored.)

Many-to-Many Relationships

Many-to-many relationships are also very common. There is, for example, a many-to-many relationship between an order placed by a Lasers Only customer and the merchandise items carried by the store. An order can contain multiple items; each item can appear on more than one order. The same is true of the orders placed with distributors. An order can contain multiple items and each item can appear on more than one order.

A many-to-many relationship exists between entities A and B if for two instances of those entities (A_i and B_i), A_i can be related to zero, one, or more instances of entity B and B$_i$ can be related to zero, one, or more instances of entity A.

Many-to-many relationships bring two major problems to a database's design. These issues and the way in which we solve them are discussed in the next major section of this chapter ("Dealing with Many-to-Many Relationships").

Weak Entities and Mandatory Relationships

As we have been discussing types of data relationships, we have defined those relationships by starting each with "zero," indicating that the participation by a given instance of an entity in a relationship is optional. For example, Lasers Only can store data about a customer in its database before the customer places an order. Therefore, an instance of the customer entity does not have to be related to any instances of the order entity.

However, the reverse is not true in this database: An order *must* be related to a customer. Without a customer, an order cannot exist. An order is therefore an example of a *weak entity*, one that cannot exist in the database unless a related instance of another entity is present and related to it. An instance of the customer entity can be related to zero, one, or more orders. However, an instance of the order entity must be related to one and only one customer. The "zero" option is not available to a weak entity. The relationship between an instance of the order entity and the customer is therefore a mandatory relationship.

Identifying weak entities and their associated mandatory relationships can be very important for maintaining the consistency and integrity of the database. Consider the effect, for example, of storing an order without knowing the customer to which it belongs. There would be no way to ship the item to the customer, causing a company to lose business.

Documenting Relationships

The Chen and Information Engineering methods of drawing ER diagrams have very different ways of representing relationships, each of which has its advantages in terms of the amount of information it provides and its complexity.

The Chen Method

The Chen method uses diamonds for relationships and lines with arrows to show the type of relationship between entities. For example, in Figure 2-5 you can see the relationship between a Lasers Only customer and an order. The single arrow pointing toward the customer entity indicates that an order belongs to at most one customer. The double arrow pointing toward the order entity indicates that a customer can place one or more orders. The word within the relationship diamond gives some indication of the meaning of the relationship.

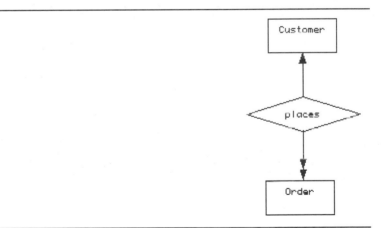

Figure 2-5: Using the Chen method with relationship diamonds and arrows

There are two alternative styles within the Chen method. The first (for example, Figure 2-6) replaces the arrows with numbers and letters. A "1" indicates that an order comes from one customer. The "M" (or an "N") indicates that a customer can place many orders.

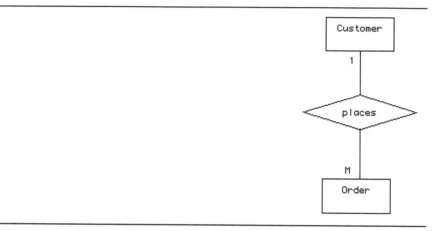

Figure 2-6:   A Chen method ER diagram using letters and numbers rather than arrows to show relationships

The second alternative addresses the problem of trying to read the relationship in both directions when the name of the relationship is within the diamond. "Customer places order" makes sense, but "order places customer" does not. To solve the problem, this alternative removes the relationship name from the diamond and adds both the relationship and its inverse to the diagram, as in Figure 2-7. This version of the diagram can be read easily in either direction: "A customer places many orders" and "An order is placed by one customer."

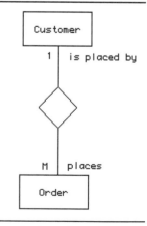

Figure 2-7:   Adding inverse relationships to a Chen method ER diagram

There is one major limitation to the Chen method of drawing ER diagrams: There is no obvious way to indicate weak entities and mandatory relationships. For example, an order should not exist in the database without a customer. Therefore, order is a weak entity and its relationship with a customer is mandatory.

Some database designers have therefore added a new symbol to the Chen method for a weak entity — a double-bordered rectangle:

Whenever a weak entity is introduced into an ER diagram, it indicates that the relationship between that entity and at least one of its parents is mandatory. However, if the entity does happen to have multiple parents, then there is no way to determine simply by looking at the diagram which of the relationships are mandatory.

The Information Engineering Method

The Information Engineering (IE) method exchanges simplicity in line ends for added information. As a first example, consider Figure 2-8. This is the same one-to-many relationship we have been using to demonstrate the Chen method ER diagrams. However, in this case the ends of the lines indicate which relationships are mandatory.

The double line below the customer entity means that each order is related to one and only one customer. Because zero is not an option, the relationship is mandatory. In contrast, the 0 and three-legged teepee connected to the order entity mean that a customer may have zero, one, or more orders.

There are four symbols used at the ends of lines in an IE diagram:

- | |: One and one only (mandatory relationship)
- 0 |: Zero or one
- > |: One or more (mandatory relationship)
- >0: Zero, one, or more

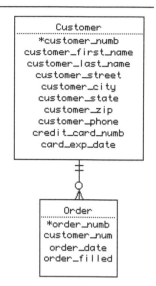

Figure 2-8:   A one-to-many relationship using the IE method

Although we often see the symbols turned 90°, as they are in Figure 2-8, they are actually readable if viewed sideways as in the preceding list.

An IE method ER diagram often includes attributes directly on the diagram. As you can see in Figure 2-8, entity identifiers are marked with an asterisk.

Basic Relationships for Lasers Only

The major entities in the Lasers Only database are diagrammed in Figure 2-9. You read the relationships in the following way:

- ♦ One customer can place zero, one, or more orders. An order comes from one and only one customer.
- ♦ An order has one or more items on it. An item can appear on zero, one, or more orders.
- ♦ An actor appears in zero, one, or more items. An item has zero, one, or more actors in it. (There may occasionally be

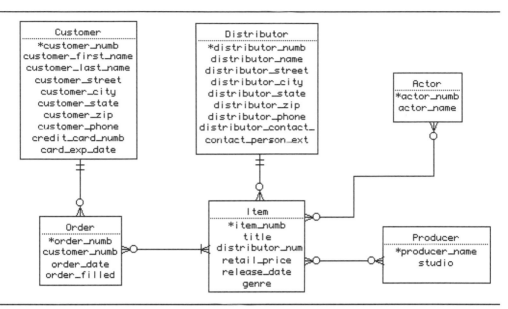

Figure 2-9:   **The major entities and the relationships between them in the Lasers Only database**

films that feature animals rather than human actors; therefore it is probably unwise to require that every merchandise item be related to at least one actor.)

♦ Each item has zero, one, or more producers. Each producer is responsible for zero, one, or more items. (Although in practice you would not store data about a producer unless that producer was related to an item, leaving the relationship between a producer and an item as optional means that you can store producers without items if necessary.)

The major thing to notice about this design is that there are three many-to-many relationships: order to item, actor to item, and producer to item. Before you can map this data model to a relational database, they must be handled in some way.

Dealing with Many-to-Many Relationships

As you read earlier, there are problems with many-to-many relationships. The first is fairly straightforward: The relational data model cannot handle many-to-many relationships directly; it is limited to one-to-one and one-to-many relationships. This means that you must replace the many-to-many relationships that you have identified in your database environment with a collection of one-to-many relationships if you want to be able to use a relational DBMS.

The second is a bit more subtle. To understand it, consider the relationship between an order Lasers Only places with a distributor and the merchandise items on the order. There is a many-to-many relationship between the order and the item because each order can be for many items and, over time, each item can appear on many orders. Whenever Lasers Only places an order for an item, the number of copies of the item varies, depending on the perceived demand for the item at the time the order is placed.

Now the question: Where should we store the quantity being ordered? It cannot be part of the order entity because the quantity depends on which item we are talking about. By the same token, the quantity cannot be part of the item entity because the quantity depends on the specific order.

What you have just seen is known as *relationship data*, data that apply to the relationship between two entities rather than to the entities themselves. Relationships, however, cannot have attributes. We therefore must have some entity to represent the relationship between the two, an entity to which the relationship data can belong.

Composite Entities

Entities that exist to represent the relationship between two other entities are known as *composite* entities. As an example of how composite entities work, consider the relationship between an order placed by a Lasers Only customer and the items on the order. There is a many-to-many relationship between an item and an order: An order can contain many items and over time the same item can appear on many orders.

What we then need is an entity that tells us that a specific title appears on a specific order. If you look at Figure 2-10, you will see three order instances and three merchandise item instances. The first order for customer 0985 contains only one item (item 0244). The second order for customer 0985 contains a second copy of item 0244 as well as item 10101. The third order, which belongs to customer 1212, also has two items on it (item 10101 and item 00250).

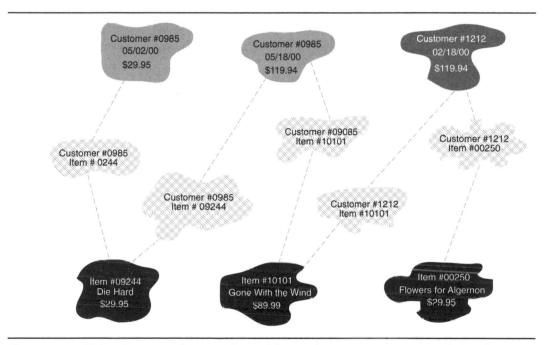

Figure 2-10: **Using instance of composite entities to change many-to-many relationships into one-to-many relationships**

There are five items ordered among the three orders. The middle of the diagram therefore contains five instances of a composite entity we will call a "line item" (thinking of it as a line item on a packing slip). The line item entity has been created solely to represent the relationship between an order and a merchandise item.

Each order is related to one line item instance for each item on the order. In turn, each item is related to one line item instance for each order on which it appears. Each line item instance is related to one and only one order; it is also related to one and only one merchandise item. As a result, the relationship between an order and its line items is one-to-many (one order has many line items) and the relationship between an item and the orders on which it appears is one-to-many (one merchandise item appears in many line items). The presence of the composite entity has removed the original many-to-many relationship and turned it into two one-to-many relationships.

If necessary, the composite entity can be used to store relationship data. In the preceding example, we might include an attribute for the quantity ordered, a flag to indicate whether it has been shipped, and a shipping date.

Documenting Composite Entities

In some extensions of the Chen method for drawing ER diagrams, the symbol for a composite entity is the combination of the rectangle used for an entity and the diamond used for a relationship:

The Information Engineering method, however, has no special symbol for a composite entity.

Resolving Lasers Only's Many-to-Many Relationships

To eliminate Lasers Only's many-to-many relationships, the database designer must replace each many-to-many relationship with a composite entity and two one-to-many relationships. As you can see in Figure 2-11, the three new entities are as follows:

- Order lines: The order lines entity represents one item appearing on one order. Each order can have many "order lines," but an order line must appear on one and only one order. By the same token, an order line contains one and only one item but the same item can appear on many order lines, each of which corresponds to a different order.
- Performance: The perfomance entity represents one actor appearing in one film. Each performance is for one and only one film although a film can have many performances (one for each actor in the film). Conversely, an actor is related to one performance for each film in which he or she appears although each performance is in one and only one film.
- Production: The production entity represents one producer working on one film. A producer may be involved in many productions, although each production relates to one and only one producer. The relationship with item indicates that each film can be produced by many producers but that each production relates to only one item.

Note: If you find sorting out the relationships in Figure 2-11 a bit difficult, keep in mind that if you rotate the up-and-down symbols 90°, you will actually be able to read the relationships.

Because composite entities exist primarily to indicate a relationship between two other entities, they must be related to both of their parent entities. This is why the relationship between each composite entity in Figure 2-11 and its parents is mandatory.

Relationships and Business Rules

In many ways, database design is as much an art as a science. Exactly what is the "correct' design for a specific business depends on the business rules; what is correct for one organization may not be correct for another.

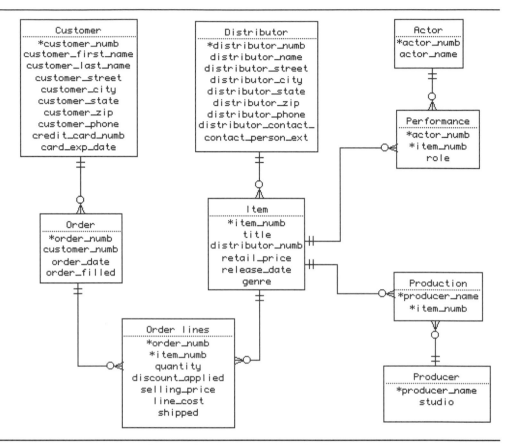

Figure 2-11:   The complete ER diagram for the Lasers Only database

As an example, assume that you are creating a database for a retail establishment that has more than one store. One of the things you are being asked to model in the database is an employee's schedule. Before you can do that, you need to answer the question of the relationship between an employee and a store: Is it one-to-many or many-to-many? Does an employee always work at only one store—in which case the relationship is one-to-many—or can an employee split his or her time between more than one store, producing a many-to-many relationship? This is not a matter of right or wrong database design, but an issue of how the business operates.

The bottom line is that no matter how much you know about database design, you will not have a good database unless the relationships depicted in that database are an accurate reflection of the relationships in the database environment.

Data Modeling versus Data Flow

One of the most common mistakes people make when they are beginning to do data modeling is to confuse data models with data flows. A *data flow* shows how data are handled within an organization, including who handles the data, where the data are stored, and what is done to the data. In contrast, a *data model* depicts the internal, logical relationships between the data, without regard to who is handling the data or what is being done with them.

Data flows are often documented in data flow diagrams. For example, in Figure 2-12 you can see a top-level data flow diagram for Lasers Only. The squares represent the people who are handling the data. Circles represent *processes*, or things that are done with the data. A place where data are stored (a *data store*) appears as two parallel lines, in this example containing the words "Main database." The arrows on the lines show the way in which data pass from one place to another.

Data flow diagrams are often exploded to show more detail. For example, Figure 2-13 contains an explosion of the "Take Order" process from Figure 2-12. You can now see that the process of taking an order involves two major steps: getting customer information and getting item information.

Each of the processes in Figure 2-13 can be exploded even further to show additional detail (see Figure 2-14 and Figure 2-15). At this point, the diagrams are almost detailed enough so that an application designer can plan an application program.

Where do the database and its ER diagram fit into all of this? The entire ER diagram is buried inside the "Main database." In fact,

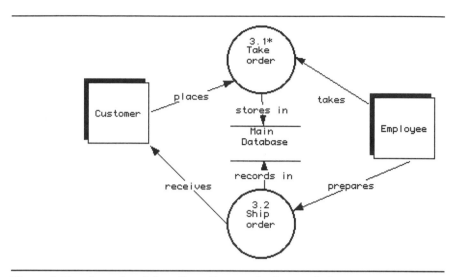

Figure 2-12:   A top-level data flow diagram for Lasers Only

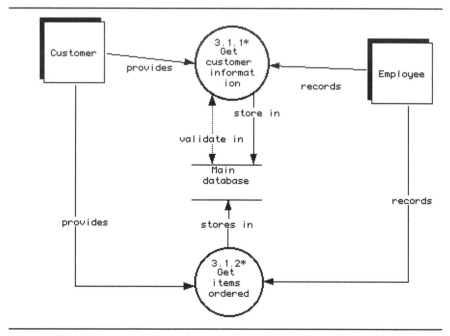

Figure 2-13:   An explosion of the Take order process from Figure 2-12

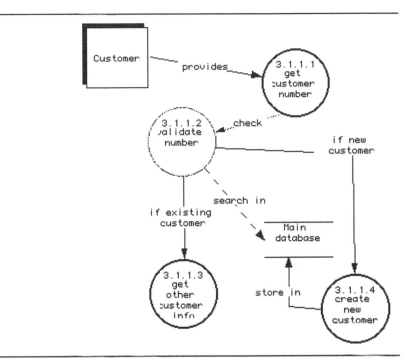

Figure 2-14:   An explosion of the "Get customer information" process from Figure 2-13

most CASE tools allow you to link your ER diagram to a database's representation on a data flow diagram. Then, you can simply double-click on the database representation to bring the ER diagram into view.

> *Note: Do not forget that you can read a great deal more about using a CASE tool in Chapter 9.*

There are a few guidelines you can use to keep data flows and data models separate:

- A data flow shows who uses or handles data. A data model does not.
- A data flow shows how data are gathered (the people or other sources from which they come). A data model does not.

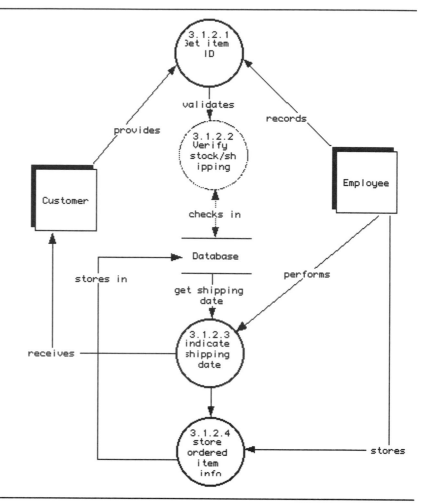

Figure 2-15: An explosion of the "Get items Oodered" process from Figure 2-13

- A data flow shows operations on data (the processes through which data are transformed). A data model does not.
- A data model shows how data entities are interrelated. A data flow does not.
- A data model shows the attributes that describe data entities. A data flow does not.

The bottom line is this: A data model contains information about the data being stored in a database (entities, attributes, and entity relationships). If data about an entity are not going to be stored in the database, then that entity should not be part of the database. For example, although the Lasers Only data flow diagram shows the Lasers Only employee who handles most of the data, no data about employees are going to be stored in the database. Therefore, there is no employee entity in the ER diagram.

Schemas

A completed entity-relationship diagram represents the overall, logical plan of a database. In database terms, it is therefore known as a *schema*. This is the way in which the people responsible for maintaining the database will see the design. However, users (both interactive users and application programs) may work with only a portion of the logical schema. And both the logical schema and the users' views of the data are at the same time distinct from the physical storage

The underlying phsyical storage, which is managed by the DBMS, is known as the *physical schema*. It is for the most part determined by the DBMS. (Only very large DBMSs give you any control over physical storage.) The beauty of this arrangement is that both database designers and users do not need to be concerned about physical storage, greatly simplifying access to the database and making it much easier to make changes to both the logical and physical schemas.

Because there are three ways to look at a database, most databases today are said to be based on a *three-schema architecture* (see Figure 2-16). Systems programmers and other people involved with managing physical storage deal with the physical schema. Database designers, database administrators, and some application programmers are aware of and use the logical schema. End users working interactively and application programmers who are creating database applications for them work with user views of the database.

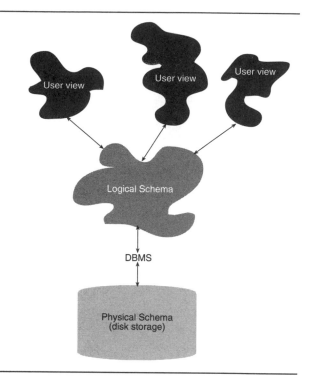

Figure 2-16:   The three-schema architecture

Throughout the rest of this book we will be focusing on the design of the logical schema. You will also learn how to create and use database elements that provide users with limited portions of the database.

For Further Reading

The entity–relationship model was developed by Peter Chen. If you want to learn more about its early forms and how the model has changed, see the following:

Chen, P. "The Entity-Relationship Model: Toward a Unified View of Data." *ACM Transactions on Database Systems.* Vol. I, No. 1, March, 1976.

Chen, P. *The Entity-Relationship Approach to Logical Database Design*. QED Information Sciences, Data Base Monograph Series, No. 6, 1977.

Chen, P. *Entity-Relationship Approach to Information Modeling*. E-R Institute, 1981.

3

The Relational Data Model

Once you have a completed ER diagram, you can translate that conceptual logical schema into the formal data model required by your DBMS. Today, most new database installations are based on the relational data model. We call databases that adhere to that model "relational databases."

> *Note: The older data models—in particular the hierarchical data model and the simple network data model—are still in use in many legacy database systems. However, it is rare to find a business creating a new one. On the other hand, the object-oriented data model is still relatively new, and although it has not replaced the relational data model and does not appear to be doing so, some new installations are either object-oriented or a combination of relational and object-oriented.*

A relational database is a database whose logical structure is made up of nothing but a collection of *relations*. Although you may have

read somewhere that a relational database has "relationships between files," nothing could be further from the truth. In this chapter, you will learn exactly what a relation is and how relations
provide representations of data relationships.

> *Note: Remember from Chapter 2 that we said that a DBMS iso-
> lates database users from physical storage. A logical data model
> therefore has absolutely nothing to do with how the data are
> stored in files on disk.*

The relational data model is the result of the work of one man —
Edgar (E. F.) Codd. During the 1960s, Dr. Codd, although trained
as a mathematician, was working with existing data models. His ex-
perience led him to believe that they were clumsy and unnatural
ways of representing data relationships. He therefore went back to
mathematical set theory and focused on the construct known as a
relation. He extended that concept to produce the relational database model, which he introduced in a seminal paper in 1970.

> *Notea: You will find the citation for Codd's original paper and
> his other writings on the relational data model in the For Fur-
> ther Reading section at the end of this chapter.*

Understanding Relations

In mathematical set theory, a *relation* is the definition of a table with
columns (*attributes*) and rows (*tuples*). (The word "table" is used
synonymously with "relation.") The definition specifies what will
be contained in each column of the table, but does not include data.
When you include rows of data, you have an *instance* of a relation,
such as the small Customers relation in Figure 3-1.

At first glance, a relation looks much like a flat file or a rectangular
portion of a spreadsheet. However, because it has its underpinnings
in mathematical set theory, a relation has some very specific characteristics that distinguish it from other rectangular ways of looking

Customer number	First name	Last name	Phone
0001	Jane	Doe	(555) 555-1111
0002	John	Doe	(555) 555-2222
0003	Jane	Smith	(555) 555-3333
0004	John	Smith	(555) 555-4444

Figure 3-1:   A sample Customers relation

at data. Each of these characteristics forms the basis of a constraint that will be enforced by the DBMS.

Columns and Column Characteristics

A column in a relation has the following properties:

♦ A name that is unique within the table: Two or more tables within the same relational schema may have columns with the same names—in fact, as you will see shortly, in some circumstances this is highly desireable—but a single table must have unique column names. When the same column name appears in more than one table and tables that contain that column are used in the same data manipulation operation, you qualify the name of the column by preceding it with the name of the table and a period, as in:

```
customers.customer_number
```

♦ A domain: The values in a column are drawn from one and only one domain. As a result, relations are said to be *column homogeneous*. In addition, every column in a table is subject to a domain constraint. Depending on your DBMS, the domain constraint may be as simple as a data type, such as integers or dates. Alternatively, your DBMS may allow you to create your own, very specific, domains that can be attached to columns.

Rows and Row Characteristics

A row in a relation has the following properties:

♦ Only one value at the intersection of a column and row: A relational does not allow multivalued attributes.

♦ Uniqueness: There are no duplicate rows in a relation.

Note: For the most part, DBMSs do not enforce the unique row constraint automatically. However, as you will see in the next bullet, there is another way to obtain the same effect.

♦ A primary key: A *primary key* is a column or combination of columns that uniquely identifies each row. As long as you have unique primary keys, you will ensure that you also have unique rows. We will look at the issue of what makes a good primary key in great depth in the next major section of this chapter.

Types of Tables

A relational database works with two types of tables. *Base tables* are relations that are actually stored in the database. These are the tables that make up your schema. However, relational operations on tables produce additional tables as their result. Such tables, which exist only in main memory, are known as *virtual tables*. Virtual tables may not be legal relations—in particular, they may have no primary key—but because virtual tables are never stored in the database, this presents no problem in terms of the overall design of the database.

Note: SQL, the language used to manage most relational DBMSs, also supports "temporary base tables." Although called base tables, temporary tables are actually virtual tables in the sense that they exist only in main memory for a short time and are never stored in the physical database.

A Notation for Relations

You will see instances of relations throughout this book used as examples. However, we do not usually include data in a relation when documenting that relation. One common way to express a relation is as follows:

```
relation_name (primary key, non_primary_key_column, …)
```

For example, the Customers relation that you saw in Figure 3-1 would be written as:

```
customers (customer_numb, first_name, last_name, phone)
```

Primary Keys

As you just read, a unique primary key makes it possible to uniquely identify every row in a table. Why is this so important? The issue is the same as with entity identifiers: You want to be able to retrieve every single piece of data you put into a database.

As far as a relational database is concerned, you should need only three pieces of information to retrieve any specific bit of data: the name of the table, the name of the column, and the primary key of the row. If primary keys are unique for every row, then we can be sure that we are retrieving exactly the row we want. If they are not unique, then we are retrieving only *some* row with the primary key value, which may not be the row containing the data for which we are searching.

Along with being unique, a primary key must not contain the value *null*. Null is a special database value meaning "unknown." It is not the same as a zero or a blank. If you have one row with a null primary key, then you are actually all right. However, the minute you introduce a second one, you have lost the property of uniquess. We therefore forbid the presence of nulls in any primary key columns. This constraint, known as *entity integrity*, will be enforced by a DBMS whenever data are entered or modified.

Selecting a good primary key can be a challenge. As you may remember from Chapter 2, some entities have natural primary keys,
such as purchase order numbers. These are arbitrary, meaningless,
unique identifiers that a company attaches to the orders it sends to
vendors and are therefore ideal primary keys.

Primary Keys to Identify People

What about a primary key to identify people? The first thing that
pops into your mind might be a social security number. Every person in the United States over the age of 12 months has one, right?
And the U.S. government assigns them so they are unique, right?
Unfortunately, the answer to both questions is "no."

The Social Security Administration has been known to give everyone in an entire town the same SSN; over time, SSNs are reused.
However, these are minor problems compared to the issue of the social security number being null.

Consider what happens at a college that uses social security numbers as student numbers when foreign students enroll. Upon entry
into the country, the foreign students do not have social security
numbers. Because primary keys cannot be null, the foreign students
cannot sign up for classes, or even be enrolled in the college, until
they have some sort of SSN.

The college's solution is to give them "fake" numbers in the format
999-999-XXXX, where XXXX is some number currently not in use.
Then, when the student receives a "real" SSN from the government,
the college supposedly replaces the fake value with the real one.
Sometimes, however, the process does not work. A graduate student
ended up with his first semester's grades being stored under the
fake SSN but the rest of his grades under his real number. (Rather
than changing the original data, someone created an entire new
transcript for the student.) When the time came to audit his transcript to see if he had satisfied all his graduation requirements, he
was told that he was missing an entire semester's worth of courses.

This example leads us to two important desirable qualities of primary keys:

- ◆ A primary key should be some value that is highly unlikely ever to be null.
- ◆ A primary key should never change.

Although social security numbers initially look like good natural identifiers, you will be much better off in the long run using arbitrary numbers for people—such as student numbers or account numbers—than relying on social security numbers.

> *Note: There is also a very important privacy issue associated with the user of SSNs in environments where no reporting of income is necessary. This has nothing to do with the design of a database but is often a significant social consideration.*

Avoiding Meaningful Primary Keys

It can be very tempting to code meaning into a primary key. For example, assume that Lasers Only wants to assign codes to its distributors rather than giving them arbitrary distributor numbers. Someone might create codes such as TLC for The Laser Club and JS for Jones Services. At first, this may seem like a good idea: The codes are short and by looking at them you can figure out which distributor they reference.

But what happens if one of the companies changes its name? Perhaps Jones Services is renamed to Jones Distribution House. Do you change the primary key of the distributor's table? Do you change the code so that it reads JDS? If the distributor's table were all that we cared about, that would be the easy solution.

However, consider that the table that describes merchandise items contains the code for the distributor so that Lasers Only can know which distributor provides the item. (You'll read a great deal more about this concept in the next major section of this chapter.) If you change the distributor code, you must change the code for every merchandise item that comes from that distributor. Without that change, Lasers Only will not be able to match the code to a distributor and get information about the distributor. It will appear that the item comes from a nonexistent distributor!

> *Note: This is precisely the problem about which you read in Chapter 1 concening Lasers Only's identifiers for their customers.*

Meaningful primary keys tend to change and therefore introduce the potential for major data inconsistencies between tables. Resist the temptation to use them at all costs. Here, then, is yet another property of a good primary key:

> ◆ A primary key should avoid using meaningful data. Use arbitrary identifiers or concatenations of arbitrary identifiers wherever possible.

It is not always possible to use completely meaningless primary keys. You may find, for example, that you need to include dates or times in primary keys to distinguish between events. The suggestion that you should not use meaningful primary keys is therefore not a hard-and-fast rule but a guideline to which you should try to adhere whenever it is realistic to do so.

Concatenated Primary Keys

Some tables have no single column in which the values never duplicate. As an example, look at the sample order lines table in Figure 3-2. Because there is more than one item on an order, order numbers are repeated; because the same item can appear on more than one order, order numbers are repeated. Therefore, neither column by iteself can serve as the table's primary key.

However, the combination of an order number and an item number *is* unique. We can therefore concatenate the two columns to form the table's primary key.

Order number	Item number	Quantity
10991	0022	1
10991	0209	2
10991	1001	1
10992	0022	1
10992	0486	1
10993	0209	1
10993	1001	2
10994	0621	1

Figure 3-2:   A sample order lines table

It is true that you could also concatenate all three columns in the table and still ensure a unique primary key. However, the quantity column is not necessary to ensure uniqueness and therefore should not be used. We now have some additional properties of a good primary key:

- ♦ A concatenated primary key should be made up of the smallest number of columns necessary to ensure the uniqueness of the primary key.
- ♦ Wherever possible, the columns used in a concatenated primary key should be meaningless identifiers.

All-Key Relations

It is possible to have a table in which every column is part of the primary key. As an example, consider a library card catalog. Each book title carried by a library has a natural unique primary key—its ISBN (International Standard Book Number). Each ISBN is assigned one or more subject headings in the library's catalog; each subject heading is also assigned to one or more books. We therefore have a many-to-many relationship between books and subject headings.

A relation to depict this relationship might be:

```
subject catalog (isbn, subject heading)
```

All we need to do is pair a subject heading with a book identifier. No additional data are needed. Therefore, all columns in the table become part of the primary key.

There is absolutely no problem with having all-key relations in a database. In fact, they occur whenever a database design contains a composite entity that has no relationship data. They are not necessarily an error and you can use them wherever needed.

Representing Data Relationships

In the preceding section we alluded to the use of identifiers in more than one relation. This is the way in which relational databases represent relationships between entities. To make this concept clearer, take a look at the three tables in Figure 3-3.

Each table in the illustration is directly analogous to the entity by the same name in the Lasers Only ER diagram. The orders table (the orders entity) is identified by an order number, an arbitrary unique primary key assigned by Lasers Only. The items table (the items entity) is identified by an item number, another arbitrary unique primary key.

The third table—line items (the line items entity)—tells the company which items are part of which order. As you saw earlier in this chapter, this table requires a concatenated primary key because multiple items can appear on multiple orders. The selection of this primary key, however, has more significance than simply uniquely identifying each row: It also represents a relationship between the line items, the orders on which they appear, and the items being ordered.

The item number column in the line items relation is the same as the primary key of the item table. This indicates a one-to-many relationship between the two tables. By the same token, there is also a one-to-many relationship between the orders and line items tables

Items

Item number	Title	Distributor number	Price
1001	Gone with the Wind	002	69.95
1002	Star Wars: Special Edition	002	39.95
1003	Die Hard	004	29.95
1004	Bambi	006	29.95

Orders

Order number	Customer number	Order date
11100	0012	12/18/00
11101	0186	12/18/00
11102	0056	12/18/00

Line items

Order number	Item number	Quantity	Shipped?
11100	1001	1	Y
11100	1002	1	Y
11101	1002	2	Y
11102	1002	1	N
11102	1003	1	N
11102	1001	1	N

Figure 3-3:   Three relations from the Lasers Only database

because the order number column in the line items table is the same as the primary key of the orders table.

When a table contains a column that is the same as the primary key of a table, the column is called a *foreign key*. The matching of foreign keys to primary keys represents data relationships in a relational database. As far as the user of a relational database is concerned, there are no structures that show relationships other than the matching columns.

> *Note: This is why the idea that relational databases have "relationships between files" is so absurd. The relationships in a relational database are between logical constructs — tables — and nothing else. Such structures make absolutely no assumptions about physical file storage.*

Foreign keys may be a part of a concatenated primary key or they may not be part of their table's primary key at all. Consider, for example, a pair of simple Lasers Only customers and orders relations:

```
customers (customer number, first name, last name, phone)
orders (order number, customer number, order date)
```

The customer number column in the orders table is a foreign key that matches the primary key of the customers table. It represents the one-to-many relationship between customers and the orders they place. However, the customer number is not part of the primary key ot its table; it is a nonkey attribute that is nonetheless a foreign key.

Technically, foreign keys need not have values unless they are part of a concatenated primary key; they can be null. However, in this particular database, Lasers Only would be in serious trouble if customer number were null: There would be no way to know which customer placed an order!

A relational DBMS uses the relationships indicated by matching data between primary and foreign keys. For example, assume that a Lasers Only employee wanted to see what titles had been ordered on order number 11102. First, the DBMS identifies the rows in the line items table that contain an order number of 11102. Then, it takes the item numbers from those rows and matches them to the item numbers in the items table. In the rows where there are matches, the DBMS finally retrieves the associated title.

Referential Integrity

The procedure described in the preceding paragraph works very well—unless for some reason there is no order number in the orders table to match a row in the order lines table. This is a very undesirable condition, because there would be no way to ship the ordered item because there would be no way to find out which customer placed the order.

The relational data model therefore enforces a constraint called *referential integrity,* which states that *every nonnull foreign key value must match an existing primary key value.* Of all the constraints on a relational database, this is probably the most important because it ensures the consistency of the cross-references among tables.

Referential integrity constraints are stored in the database and enforced automatically by the DMBS. As with all other constraints, each time a user enters or modifies data, the DBMS checks the constraints and verifies that they are met. If the constraints are violated, the data modification will not be allowed.

Foreign Keys and Primary Keys in the Same Table

Foreign keys do not necessarily need to reference a primary key in a different table; they need only reference a primary key. As an example, consider the following employee relation:

```
employee (employee ID, first name, last name, department, manager ID)
```

A manager is also an employee. Therefore, the manager ID, although named differently from the employee ID, is actually a foreign key that references the primary key of its own table. The DBMS will therefore always ensure that whenever a user enters a manager ID, that manager already exists in the table as an employee.

Views

The people responsible for developing a database schema and those who write application programs for use by technologically unsophisticated users typically have knowledge of and access to the entire schema, including direct access to the database's base tables. However, it is usually undesirable to have end users working directly with base tables, primarily for security reasons.

The relational data model therefore includes a way to provide end users with their own window into the database, one that hides the details of the overall database design and prohibits direct access to the base tables.

The View Mechanism

A view is not stored with data. Instead, it is stored under a name in the data dictionary along with a database query that will retrieve its data. A view can therefore contain data from more than one table, selected rows, and selected columns.

The real beauty of storing views in this way, however, is that whenever the user includes the name of the view in a data manipulation language statement, the DBMS executes the query associated with the view name and recreates the view's table. This means that the data in a view will always be current.

A view table remains in main memory only for the duration of the data manipulation statement in which it was used. As soon as the user issues another query, the view table is removed from main meory to be replaced by the result of the most recent query.

> *Note: Some end user DBMSs give the user the ability to save the contents of a view as a base table. This is a particularly undesirable feature, as there are no provisions for automatically updating the data in the saved view table whenever the tables on which it was based change. The view table will therefore quickly become out of date and inaccurate.*

Why Use Views?

There are three good reasons to include views in the design of a database:

- ◆ As mentioned earlier, views provide a significant security mechanism by restricting users from viewing portions of a schema to which they should not have access.
- ◆ Views can simplify the design of a database for technologically unsophisticated users.
- ◆ Because views are stored as named queries, they can be used to store frequently used, complex queries. The queries can then be executed by using the name of the view in a simple query.

Like other structural elements in a relational database, views can be created and destroyed at any time. However, because views do not contain stored data, but only specification of a query that will generate a virtual table, adding or removing view definitions has no impact on base tables or the data they contain. Removing a view will create problems only when that view is used in an application program and the program is not modified to work with a different view or base table.

The Data Dictionary

The structure of a relational database is stored in the database's *data dictionary*, or *catalog*. The data dictionary is made up of a set of relations, identical in properties to the relations used to hold data. They can be queried using the same tools used to query data-handling relations. No user can modify the data dictionary tables directly. However, data manipulation language commands that create and destroy database structural elements work by modifying rows in data dictionary tables.

You will typically find the following types of information in a data dictionary:

+ Defintions of the columns that make up each table.
+ Integrity constraints placed on relations.
+ Security information (which user has the right to perform which operation of which table).
+ Definitions of other database structural elements, such as views (discussed further in Chapter 7) and user-defined domains.

When a user attempts to access data in any way, a relational DBMS first goes to the data dictionary to determine whether the database elements the user has requested are actually part of the schema. In addition, the DBMS verifies that the user has the access rights to whatever he or she is requesting.

When a user attempts to modify data, the DBMS also goes to the data dictionary to look for integrity constraints that may have been placed on the relation. If the data meet the constraints, the modification is permitted. Otherwise, the DBMS returns an error message and does not make the change.

Because all access to a relational database is through the data dictionary, relational DBMSs are said to be *data dictionary driven*.

Sample Data Dictionary Tables

The precise tables that make up a data dictionary depend somewhat on the DBMS. In this section you will see one example of a typical way in which one specific DBMS (Sybase SQL Anywhere) organizes its data dictionary.

The linchpin of the data dictionary is actually a table that documents all the data dictionary tables (syscatalog, the first few rows of which can be found in Figure 3-4). From the names of the data dictionary tables, you can probably guess that there are tables to store data about base tables, their columns, their indexes, and their foreign keys.

creator	tname	dbspace	tabletype	ncols	primary_key
SYS	SYSTABLE	SYSTEM	TABLE	12	Y
SYS	SYSCOLUMN	SYSTEM	TABLE	14	Y
SYS	SYSINDEX	SYSTEM	TABLE	8	Y
SYS	SYSIXCOL	SYSTEM	TABLE	5	Y
SYS	SYSFOREIGNKEY	SYSTEM	TABLE	8	Y
SYS	SYSFKCOL	SYSTEM	TABLE	4	Y
SYS	SYSFILE	SYSTEM	TABLE	3	Y
SYS	SYSDOMAIN	SYSTEM	TABLE	4	Y
SYS	SYSUSERPERM	SYSTEM	TABLE	10	Y
SYS	SYSTABLEPERM	SYSTEM	TABLE	11	Y
SYS	SYSCOLPERM	SYSTEM	TABLE	6	Y

Figure 3-4:   A portion of a syscatalog table

The syscatalog table describes the columns in each table (including the database dictionary tables). In Figure 3-5, for example, you can see a portion of a syscolumns table that describes the Lasers Only merchandise items table.

creator	Cname	Tname	Coltype	Nulls	Lenth	InPrimaryKey	Colno
DBA	item_numb	items	integer	N	4	Y	1
DBA	title	items	varchar	Y	60	N	2
DBA	distributor_numb	items	integer	Y	4	N	3
DBA	release_date	items	date	Y	6	N	4
DBA	retail_price	items	numeric	Y	6	N	5

Figure 3-5:   Selected rows from a syscolumns table

Keep in mind that these data dictionary tables have the same structure and must adhere to the same rules as base tables. They must have nonnull unique primary keys; they must also enforce referential integrity among themselves.

For Further Reading

If you want to follow the history of Codd's specifications for relational database, consult the following:

Codd, E. F. "A Relational Model of Data for Large Shared Databanks." *Communications of the ACM*, Vol. 13, No. 6, June, 1970.

Codd, E. F. "Extending the Relational Model to Capture More Meaning." *Transactions on Database Systems*, Vol. 4, No. 4, December, 1979.

Codd, E. F. "Relational Database: A Practical Foundation for Productivity." *Communications of the ACM*, Vol. 25, No. 2, February, 1982.

Codd, E. F. "Is Your DBMS Really Relational?" *Computerworld*, October 14, 1985: ID/1–ID/9.

Codd, E. F. *The Relational Data Model, Version 2.* Addison-Wesley, 1989.

4

Normalization

Given any pool of entities and attributes, there is a large number of
ways you can group them into relations. In this chapter, you will be
introduced to the process of *normalization*, through which you create relations that avoid most of the problems that arise from bad relational design.

There are at least two ways to approach normalization. The first is
to work from an ER diagram. If the diagram is drawn correctly, then
there are some simple rules you can use to translate it into relations
that will avoid most relational design problems. The drawback to
this approach is that it can be difficult to determine whether your
design is correct. The second approach is to use the theortical concepts behind good design to create your relations. This is a bit more
difficult than working from an ER diagram, but often results in a
better design.

In practice, you may find it useful to use a combination of both approaches. First, create an ER diagram and use it to design your relations. Then, check those relations against the theoretical rules for good design.

Translating an ER Diagram into Relations

An ER diagram in which all many-to-many relationships have been transformed into one-to-many relationships through the introduction of composite entities can be translated directly into a set of relations. To do so:

- Create one table for each entity.
- For each entity that is only at the "one" end of one or more relationships, and not at the "many" end of any relationship, create a single-column primary key, using an arbitrary unique number if no natural primary key is available.
- For each entity that is at the "many" end of one or more relationships, include the primary key of each parent entity (those at the "one" end of the relationships) in the table as foreign keys.
- If an entity at the "many" end of one or more relationships has a natural primary key (for example, an order or invoice number), use that single column as the primary key. Otherwise, concatenate the primary key of its parent or parents with any other column or columns needed for uniqueness to form the table's primary key.

Following these guidelines, we end up with the following tables for the Lasers Only database:

```
customer (customer_numb, customer_first_name, customer_last_name,
    customer_street, customer_city, customer_state, customer_zip,
    customer_phone, credit_card_numb, card_exp_date)
item (item_numb, title, distributor_numb, retail_price,
    release_date, genre)
order (order_numb, customer_numb, order_date, order_filled)
```

```
order_lines (order numb, item numb, quantity, discount_applied,
    selling_price, line_cost, shipped)
distributor (distributor numb, distributor_name,
    distributor_street, distributor_city, distributor_city,
    distributor_state, distributor_zip, distributor_phone,
    distributor_contact_person, contact_person_ext)
actor (actor numb, actor_name)
performance (actor numb, item numb, role)
producer (producer name, studio)
production (producer name, item numb)
```

> *Note: You will see these relations reworked a bit throughout the remainder of the first part of this book to help illustrate various aspects of database design. However, the preceding is the design that results from a direct translation of the ER diagram.*

Normal Forms

The theoretical rules that the design of a relation meet are known as *normal forms*. Each normal form represents an increasingly stringent set of rules. Theoretically, the higher the normal form, the better the design of the relation.

As you can see in Figure 4-1, there are six nested normal forms, indicating that if a relation is in one of the higher, inner normal forms, it is also in all of the normal forms below it.

In most cases, if you can place your relations in third normal form (3NF), then you will have avoided most of the problems common to bad relational designs. Boyce-Codd (BCNF) and fourth normal form (4NF) handle special situations that arise only occasionally. However, they are conceptually easy to understand and can be used in practice if the need arises.

Fifth normal form (5NF), however, is a complex set of criteria that is extremely difficult to work with. It is , for example, very difficult to verify that a relation is in 5NF. Most practitioners do not bother with 5NF, knowing that if their relations are in 3NF (or 4NF if the situation warrants), then their designs are generally problem free.

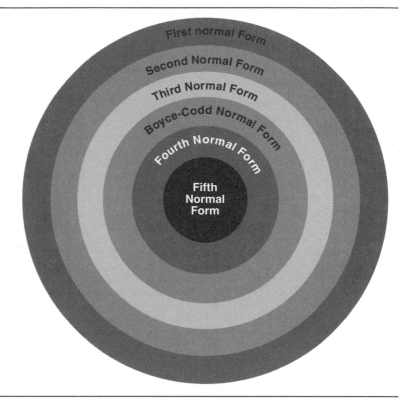

Figure 4-1:   Nested normal forms

Note: In addition to the six normal forms in Figure 4-1, there is another normal form — domain/key normal form — that is of purely theoretical importance and, to this date, has not been used as a practical design objective.

First Normal Form

A table is in first normal form (1NF) if it meets the following criteria:

The data are stored in a two-dimensional table with no repeating groups.

The key to understanding 1NF is therefore understanding the nature of a repeating group of data.

Understanding Repeating Groups

A *repeating group* is an attribute that has more than one value in each row. For example, assume that you were working with an employees relation and needed to store the names and birthdates of the employees' children. Because each employee can have more than one child, the names of children and the children's birthdates each form a repeating group.

> *Note: A repeating group is directly analogous to a multivalued attribute in an ER diagram.*

There is actually a very good reason why repeating groups are disallowed. To see what might happen if they were present, take a look at Figure 4-2, an instance of the employees relation we were just discussing.

Emp. ID	First	Last	Children's Names	Children's Birthdates
1001	Jane	Doe	Mary, Sam	1/1/92, 5/15/94
1002	John	Doe	Mary, Sam	1/1/92, 5/15/94
1003	Jane	Smith	John, Pat, Lee, Mary	10/5/94, 10/12/90, 6/6/96, 8/21/94
1004	John	Smith	Michael	7/4/96
1005	Jane	Jones	Edward, Martha	10/21/95, 10/15/89

Figure 4-2:   A relation with repeating groups

Notice that there are multiple values in a single row in both the children's names and children's birthdates columns. The two major problems this presents are:

♦ There is no way to know exactly which birthdate belongs to which child. It is tempting to say that we can associate the birthdates with the children by their positions in the list, but there is nothing to ensure that the relative positions will always be maintained.

◆ Searching the table is very difficult. If, for example, we want to know which employees have children born before 1995, the DBMS will need to perform data manipulations to extract the individual dates from the birthdates column before it can evaluate the dates themselves. Given that there is no way to know how many birthdates there are in the column for any specific row, the processing overload for searching becomes even greater.

The solution to these problems is, of course, to get rid of the repeating groups altogether.

Handling Repeating Groups

There are two ways to get rid of repeating groups to bring a relation into conformance with the rules for first normal form — a right way and a wrong way. We will first look at the wrong way so you will know what *not* to do.

In Figure 4-3 you can see a relation that handles repeating groups by creating multiple columns for the multiple values. This particular example includes three pairs of columns for a child's name and birthdate.

Emp. ID	First	Last	Child Name 1	Child B_date 1	Child Name 2	Child B_date 2	Child Name 3	Child B_date 3
1001	Jane	Doe	Mary	1/1/92	Sam	5/15/94		
1002	John	Doe	Mary	1/1/92	Sam	5/15/94		
1003	Jane	Smith	John	10/5/94	Pat	10/12/90	Lee	6/6/96
1004	John	Smith	Michael	7/4/96				
1005	Jane	Jones	Edward	10/21/95	Martha	10/15/89		

Figure 4-3:   A relation handling repeating groups in the wrong way

The relation in Figure 4-3 does meet the criteria for first normal form: The repeating groups are gone and there is no problem identifying which birthdate belongs to which child. However, the design has introduced several problems of its own:

♦ The relation is limited to three children for any given employee. This means that there is no room to store Jane Smith's fourth child. Should you put another row for Jane Smith into the table? If so, then the primary key of this relation can no longer be just the employee ID. The primary key must include at least one child's name as well.

♦ The relation wastes space for people who have less than three children. Given that disk space is one of the least expensive elements of a database system, this is probably the least of the problems with this relation.

♦ Searching for a specific child becomes very clumsy. To answer the question "Does anyone have a child named Lee?" the DBMS must construct a query that includes a search of all three child name columns because there is no way to know in which column the name might be found.

The right way to handle repeating groups is to create another table (another entity) to handle multiple instances of the repeating group. In the example we have been using, we would create a second table for the children, producing something like Figure 4-4.

Neither of the two new tables contains any repeating groups, and this form of the design avoids all the problems of the preceding solution:

♦ There is no limit to the number of children that can be stored for a given employee. To add another child, you simply add another row to the table.

♦ There is no wasted space. The children table uses space only for data that are present.

♦ Searching for a specific child is much easier because the child's name is found in only one column.

Employees

Emp. ID	First	Last
1001	Jane	Doe
1002	John	Doe
1003	Jane	Smith
1004	John	Smith
1005	Jane	Jones

Children

Emp. ID	Child Name	Birthdate
1001	Mary	1/1/92
1001	Sam	5/15/94
1002	Mary	1/1/92
1002	Sam	5/15/94
1003	John	10/5/94
1003	Pat	10/12/90
1003	Lee	6/6/96
1003	Mary	8/21/94
1004	Michael	7/4/96
1005	Edward	10/21/95
1005	Martha	10/15/89

Figure 4-4:   The correct way to handle the repeating group

Problems with First Normal Form

Although first normal form relations have no repeating groups, they are full of other problems. To see what those problems are, we will look at the relation underlying the data entry form in Chapter 1. Expressed in the notation for relations that we have been using, the relation is:

```
orders (customer number, first name, last name, street, city, state,
    zip, phone, order date, item number, title, price, has shipped)
```

The first thing we need to do is determine the primary key for this table. The customer number alone will not be sufficient because the customer number repeats for every item ordered by the customer. The item number will also not suffice, because it is repeated for every order on which it appears. We cannot use the order number because it is repeated for every item on the order. The only solution is a concatenated key, in this the combination of the order number and the item number.

Given that the primary key is comprised of the order number and the item number, there are two important things we cannot do with this relation:

- ◆ We cannot add data about a customer until the customer places at least one order because without an order and an item on that order, we do not have a complete primary key.
- ◆ We cannot add data about a merchandise item we are carrying without that item being ordered. There must be an order number to complete the primary key.

The preceding are *insertion anomalies*, a situation that arises when you are prevented from inserting data into a relation because a complete primary key is not available. (Remember that no part of a primary key can be null.)

> Note: To be strtictly correct, there is a third insertion anomaly in the orders relation: You cannot insert an order until you know one item on the order. In a practical sense, however, no one would enter an order without there being an item ordered.

Insertion anomalies are common in first normal form relations that are not also in any of the higher normal forms. In practical terms, they occur because there are data about more than one entity in the relation. The anomaly forces you to insert data about an unrelated entity (for example, a merchandise item) when you want to insert data about another entity (such as a customer).

First normal form relations can also give us problems when we delete data. Consider, for example, what happens if a customer cancels the order of a single item:

◆ In cases where the deleted item was the only item on the order, you lose all data about the order.
◆ In cases where the order was the only order on which the item appeared, you lose data about the item.
◆ In cases where the deleted item was the only item ordered by a customer, you lose all data about the customer.

These *deletion anomalies* occur because part of the primary key of a row becomes null when the merchandise item data are deleted, forcing you to remove the entire row. The result of a deletion anomaly is the loss of data that you would like to keep. In practical terms, you are forced to remove data about an unrelated entity when you delete data about another entity in the same table.

> Note: Moral to the story: More than one entity in a table is a very bad thing.

There is a final type of anomaly in the orders relation that is not related to the primary key: a *modification*, or *update*, anomaly. The orders relation has a great deal of unnecessary duplicated data, in particular information about customers. When a customer moves, then the customer's data must be changed in every row, for every item on every order ever placed by the customer. If every row is not changed correctly, then data that should be the same are no longer the same. The potential for these inconsistent data is the modification anomaly.

Second Normal Form

The solution to anomalies in a first normal form relation is to break the relation down so that there is one relation for each entity in the 1NF relation. The orders relation, for example, will break down into four relations (customers, merchandise items, orders, and line items). Such relations are in at least second normal form (2NF).

In theoretical terms, second normal form is defined as follows:

> The relation is in first normal form and all nonkey attributes are functionally dependent on the entire primary key.

The new term in the preceding is *functionally dependent,* a special relationship between attributes.

Understanding Functional Dependencies

A functional dependency is a one-way relationship between two attributes such that at any given time, for each unique value of attribute A, only one value of attribute B is associated with it through the relation. For example, assume that A is the customer number from the orders relation. Each customer number is associated with one customer first name, one last name, one street address, one city, one state, one zip code, and one phone number. Although the values for those attributes may change, at any moment, there is only one.

We therefore can say that first name, last name, street, city, state, zip, and phone are functionally dependent upon the customer number. This relationship is often written

```
customer number -> first name, last name, street, city, state, zip,
    phone
```

and read "customer number determines first name, last name, street, city, state, zip, and phone." In this relationship, customer number is known as the *determinant* (an attribute that determines the value of other attributes).

Notice that the functional dependency does not necessarily hold in the reverse direction. For example, any given first or last name may be associated with more than one customer number. (It would be unusual to have a customer table of any size without some repetition of names.)

The function dependencies in the orders table are:

```
customer number -> first name, last name, street, city, state, zip,
    phone
item number -> title, price
order number -> customer number, order date
item number + order number -> has shipped
```

Notice first that there is one determinant for each entity in the relation and that the determinant is what we have chosen as the entity identifier. Notice also that when an entity has a concatenated identifier, the determinant is also concatenated. In this example, whether an item has shipped depends on the combination of the item and the order.

Using Functional Dependencies to Reach 2NF

If you have correctly identified the functional dependencies among the attributes in a database environment, then you can use them to create second normal form relations. Each determinant becomes the primary key of a relation. All the attributes that are functionally dependent upon it become nonkey attributes in the relation.

The four relations into which the original orders relation should be broken are:

```
customers (customer number, first name, last name, street, city,
    state, zip, phone)
items (item number, title, price)
orders (order number, customer number, order date)
line items (order number, item number, has shipped)
```

Each of these should in turn correspond to a single entity in your ER diagram.

> Note: When it comes to deciding what is driving database design — functional dependencies or entities — it is really a "chicken and egg" situation. What is most important is that

there is consistency between the ER diagram and the functional dependencies you identify in your relations. It makes no difference whether you design by looking for functional dependencies or for entities.

The relations we have created from the original orders relation have eliminated the anomalies present in the original:

- It is now possible to insert data about a customer before the customer places an order.
- It is now possible to insert data about an order before we know an item on the order.
- It is now possible to store data about merchandise items before they are ordered.
- Line items can be deleted from an order without affecting data describing that item, the order itself, or the merchandise item.
- Data describing the customer are stored only once and therefore any change to those data need to be made only once. A modification anomaly cannot occur.

Problems with 2NF Relations

Although second normal form eliminates problems from many relations, you will occasionally run into relations that are in second normal form yet still exhibit anomalies. Assume, for example, that each laser disc title that Lasers Only carries comes from one distributor and that each distributor has only one warehouse, which has only one phone number. The following relation is therefore in second normal form:

```
items (item number, title, distributor, warehouse phone number)
```

For each item number, there is only one value for the item's title, distributor, and warehouse phone number. However, there is one insertion anomaly—you cannot insert data about a distributor until you have an item from that distributor—and a deletion anomaly— if you delete the only item from a distributor, you lose data about the distributor. There is also a modification anomaly: The distributor's warehouse phone number is duplicated for every item the company gets from that distributor. The relation is in second normal form, but not third.

Third Normal Form

Third normal form is designed to handle situations like the one you just read about in the preceding section. In terms of entities, the items relation does contain two entities: the merchandise item and the distributor. That alone should convince you that the relation needs to broken down into two smaller relations, both of which are now in third normal form:

```
items (item number, distributor)
distributors (distrbutor, warehouse phone number)
```

The theoretical definition of normal form says:

> The relation is in second normal form and there are no transitive dependencies.

The functional dependencies found in the original relation are an example of a *transitive dependency*.

Transitive Dependencies

A transitive dependency exists when you have the following functional dependency pattern:

```
A -> B and B - > C therefore A -> C
```

This is precisely the case with the original items relation. The only reason that the warehouse phone number is functionally dependent on the item number is because the distributor is functionally dependent on the item number and the phone number is functionally dependent on the distributor. The functional dependencies are really:

```
item number -> distributor
distributor -> warehouse phone number
```

> *Note: Transitive dependencies take their name from the transitive property in mathematics, which states that if a > b and b > c, then a > c.*

There are two determinants in the original items relation, each of which should be the primary key of its own relation. However, it is not merely the presence of the second determinant that creates the transitive dependency. What really matters is that the second determinant is not a candidate key for the relation.

Consider, for example, this relation:

```
items (item number, UPC code, distributor, price)
```

The item number is an arbitrary value that Lasers Only assigns to each merchandise item. The UPC code is an industry-wide code that is unique to each item as well. The functional dependencies in this relation are:

```
item number -> UPC code, distributor, price
UPC code -> item number, distributor, price
```

Is there a transitive dependency here? No, because the second determinant is a candidate key. (Lasers Only could just as easily have used the UPC code as the primary key.) There are no insertion, deletion, or modification anomalies in this relation; it describes only one entity — the merchandise item.

A transitive dependency therefore exists only when the determinant that is not the primary key is not a candidate key for the relation.

When you have a transitive dependency in a 2NF relation, you should break the relation into two smaller relations, each of which has one of the determinants in the transitive dependency as its primary key. The attributes determined by the determinants become the nonkey attributes in each relation. This removes the transitive dependency—and its associated anomalies—and places the relations in third normal form.

> *Note: A second normal form relation that has no transitive dependencies is, of course, automatically in third normal form.*

Boyce–Codd Normal Form

For most relations, third normal form is a good design objective. Relations in that state are free of most anomalies. However, occasionally you run across relations that exhibit special characteristics where anomalies still occur. Boyce–Codd normal form (BCNF) and fourth normal form (4NF) were created to handle such special situations.

> *Note: If your relations are in third normal form and do not exhibit the special characteristics that BCNF and 4NF were designed to handle, then they are automatically in 4NF.*

The easiest way to understand BCNF is to start with an example. Assume that Lasers Only decides to add a relation to its database to handle employee work scheduling. Each employee works one or two 4-hour shifts a day at the store. During each shift, an employee is assigned to one station (a place in the store, such as the front desk or the stockroom). Only one employee works a station during a given shift.

A relation to handle the schedule might be designed as the following:

```
schedule (employee ID, date, shift, station, worked shift?)
```

Given the rules for the scheduling (one person per station per shift), there are two possible primary keys for this relation: employee ID + date + shift or date + shift + station. The functional dependencies in the relation are:

```
employee ID + date + shift -> station, worked shift?
date + shift + station -> employee ID, worked shift?
```

Keep in mind that this holds true only because there is only one person working each station during each shift.

> *Note: There is very little difference between the two candidate keys as far as the choice of a primary key is concerned. In cases like this, you can choose either one.*

This schedule relation exhibits overlapping concatenated candidate keys. (Both candidate keys have date and shift in common.) Boyce–Codd normal form was designed to deal with relations that exhibit this characteristic.

To be in Boyce–Codd normal form, a relation must meet the following rule:

> The relation is in third normal form and all determinants are candidate keys.

BCNF is considered to be a more general way of looking at 3NF because it includes those relations with the overlapping candidate keys. The sample schedule relation we have been considering does meet the criteria for BCNF because the two determinants are indeed candidate keys.

Fourth Normal Form

Like BCNF, fourth normal form was designed to handle relations that exhibit a special characteristic that does not arise too often. In this case, the special characteristic is something known as a *multi-valued dependency.*

As an example, consider the following relation:

```
movie info (title, star, producer)
```

A given movie can have more than one star; it can also have more than one producer. The same star can appear in more than one movie; the producer can also work on more than one movie (for example, see the instance in Figure 4-5). The relation must therefore include all columns in its key.

Title	Star	Producer
Great Film	Lovely Lady	Money Bags
Great Film	Handsome Man	Money Bags
Great Film	Lovely Lady	Helen Pursestrings
Great Film	Handsome Man	Helen Pursestrings
Boring Movie	Lovely Lady	Helen Pursestrings
Boring Movie	Precocious Child	Helen Pursestrings

Figure 4-5:   A relation with a multivalued dependency

Because there are no nonkey attributes, this relation is in BCNF. Nonetheless, the relation exhibits anomalies:

- You cannot insert the stars of a movie without knowing at least one producer.
- You cannot insert the producer of a movie without knowing at least one star.
- If you delete the only producer from a movie, you lose information about its stars.
- If you delete the only star from a movie, you lose information about its producers.
- Each producer's name is duplicated for every star in the move. By the same token, each star's name is duplicated for each producer of the movie. This unnecessary duplication forms the basis of a modification anomaly.

There are at least two unrelated entities in this relation, one that handles the relationship between a movie and its stars and another that handles the relationship between a movie and its producers. In a practical sense, that is the cause of the anomalies. (Arguably, there are also movie, star, and producer entities involved.)

However, in theoretical terms, the anomalies are caused by the presence of a multivalued dependency in the same relation, which must be eliminated to go to fourth normal form. The rule for fourth normal form is:

The relation is in Boyce–Codd normal form and there are no multivalued dependencies.

Multivalued Dependencies

A multivalued dependency exists when for each value of attribute A, there exists a finite set of values of attribute B that are associated with it and a finite set of values of attribute C that are also associated with it. Attributes B and C are independent of each other.

In the example we have been using, there is just such a dependency. First, for each movie title, there is a group of actors (the stars) who are associated with the movie. For each title, there is also a group of producers who are associated with it. However, the actors and the producers are independent of one another.

> Note: At this point, do not let semantics get in the way of database theory. Yes, it is true that producers fund the movies in which the actors are starring, but in terms of database relationships, there is no direct connection between the two.

The multivalued dependency can be written:

```
title ->> star
title ->> producer
```

and read "title multidetermines star and title multidetermines producer."

> Note: To be strictly accurate, a functional dependency is a special case of a multivalued dependency where what is being determined is one value rather than a group of values.

To eliminate the multivalued dependency and bring this relation into fourth normal form, you split the relation, placing each part of the dependency in its own relation:

```
movie stars (title, star)
movie producers (title, producer)
```

With this design, you can independently insert and remove stars and producers without affecting the other. Star and producer names also appear only once for each movie with which they are involved.

Normalized Relations and Database Performance

Normalizing the relations in a database separates entities into their own relations and makes it possible for you to enter, modify, and delete data without disturbing entities other than the one directly being modified. However, normalization is not without its downside.

When you split relations so that relationships are represented by matching primary and foreign keys, you force the DBMS to perform matching operations between relations whenever a query requires data from more than one table. The operation typically used is known as a *join*.

In theory, a join looks for rows with matching values between two tables and creates a new row in a result table every time it finds a match. In practice, however, performing a join involves manipulating more data than the simple combination of the two tables being joined would suggest. Joins of large tables (those of more than a few hundred rows) can significantly slow down the performance of a DBMS.

To understand what can happen, you need to know something about the relational algebra join operation. (Relational algebra is a set of operations used to manipulate and extract data from relations.) As with all relational algebra operations, the result of a join is a new table.

Equi-Joins

In its most common form, a join forms new rows when data in the two source tables match. Because we are looking for rows with equal values, this type of join is known as an *equi-join* (or a *natural equi-join*). As an example, consider the two tables in Figure 4-6.

Notice that the ID number column is the primary key of the customers table and that the same column is a foreign key in the orders

```
customers

ID number first name   last name

001          Jane        Doe
002          John        Doe
003          Jane        Smith
004          John        Smith
005          Jane        Jones
006          John        Jones


orders

order number  ID number  order date   order total

001            002         10/10/99       250.65
002            002          2/21/00       125.89
003            003         11/15/99      1567.99
004            004         11/22/99       180.92
005            004         12/15/99       565.00
006            006         10/8/99         25.00
007            006         11/12/99        85.00
008            006         12/29/99       109.12
```

Figure 4-6:   Two tables with a primary key–foreign key relationship

table. The ID number column in orders therefore serves to relate orders to the customers to which they belong.

Assume that you want to see the names of the customers who placed each order. To do so, you must join the two tables, creating combined rows wherever there is a matching ID number. In database terminology, we are joining the two tables *over* ID number. The result table can be found in Figure 4-7.

An equi-join can begin with either source table. (The result should be the same regardless of the direction in which the join is performed.) The join compares each row in one source table with the rows in the second. For each row in the first source table that matches data in the second source table in the column or columns over which the join is being performed, a new row is placed in the result table.

```
result_table

ID number first_name    last_name      order_numb   order_date   order_total

002        John         Doe            001          10/10/99         250.65
002        John         Doe            002           2/21/00         125.89
003        Jane         Smith          003          11/15/99        1597.99
004        John         Smith          004          11/22/99         180.92
004        John         Smith          005          12/15/99         565.00
006        John         Jones          006          10/8/99           25.00
006        John         Jones          007          11/12/99          85.00
006        John         Jones          008          12/29/99         109.12
```

Figure 4-7:   The joined table

Assuming that we are using the customers table as the first source table, producing the result table in Figure 4-7 might therefore proceed conceptually as follows:

1. Search orders for rows with an ID number of 001. Because there are no matching rows in orders, do not place a row in the result table.

2. Search orders for rows with an ID number of 002. There are two matching rows in orders. Create two new rows in the result table, placing the same customer information at the end of each row in orders.

3. Search orders for rows with an ID number of 003. There is one matching row in orders. Place one new row in the result table.

4. Search orders for rows with an ID number of 004. There are two matching rows in orders. Place two rows in the result table.

5. Search orders for rows with an ID number of 005. There are no matching rows in orders. Therefore do not place a row in the result table.

6. Search orders for rows with an ID number of 006. There are three matching rows in orders. Place three rows in the result table.

Notice that if an ID number does not appear in both tables, then no row is placed in the result table. This behavior categorizes this type of join as an *inner join*.

What's Really Going On: PRODUCT and RESTRICT

From a relational algebra point of view, a join can be implemented using two other operations: product and restrict. As you will see, this sequence of operations requires the manipulation of a great deal of data and, if implemented by a DBMS, can result in very slow query performance.

The restrict operation retrieves rows from a table by matching each row against logical criteria (a *predicate*). Those rows that meet the criteria are placed in the result table; those that do not meet the criteria are omitted.

The product operation (the mathematical Cartesian product) makes every possible pairing of rows from two source tables. In Figure 4-8, for example, the product of the customers and orders tables produces a result table with 48 rows (the six customers times the eight orders). The ID number column appears twice because it is a part of both source tables.

> Note: Although 48 rows may not seem like a lot, consider the size of a product table created from tables with 100 and 1000 rows! The manipulation of a table of this size can tie up a lot of disk I/O and CPU time.

In some rows, the ID number is the same. These are the rows that would have been included in a join. We can therefore apply a restrict predicate to the product table to end up with the same table provided by the join you saw earlier. The predicate's logical condition can be written:

```
customers.id_numb = orders.id_numb
```

The rows that are selected by this predicate appear in black in Figure 4-9; those eliminated by the predicate are in gray. Notice that the black rows are exactly the same as those in the result table of the join (Figure 4-7).

product_table

ID number (Customers)	first name	last name	ID number (Orders)	order number	order date	order total
001	Jane	Doe	002	001	10/10/99	250.65
001	Jane	Doe	002	002	2/21/00	125.89
001	Jane	Doe	003	003	11/15/99	1597.99
001	Jane	Doe	004	004	11/22/99	180.92
001	Jane	Doe	004	005	12/15/99	565.00
001	Jane	Doe	006	006	10/8/99	25.00
001	Jane	Doe	006	007	11/12/99	85.00
001	Jane	Doe	006	008	12/29/99	109.12
002	John	Doe	002	001	10/10/99	250.65
002	John	Doe	002	002	2/21/00	125.89
002	John	Doe	003	003	11/15/99	1597.99
002	John	Doe	004	004	11/22/99	180.92
002	John	Doe	004	005	12/15/99	565.00
002	John	Doe	006	006	10/8/99	25.00
002	John	Doe	006	007	11/12/99	85.00
002	John	Doe	006	008	12/29/99	109.12
003	Jane	Smith	002	001	10/10/99	250.65
003	Jane	Smith	002	002	2/21/00	125.89
003	Jane	Smith	003	003	11/15/99	1597.99
003	Jane	Smith	004	004	11/22/99	180.92
003	Jane	Smith	004	005	12/15/99	565.00
003	Jane	Smith	006	006	10/8/99	25.00
003	Jane	Smith	006	007	11/12/99	85.00
003	Jane	Smith	006	008	12/29/99	109.12
004	John	Smith	002	001	10/10/99	250.65
004	John	Smith	002	002	2/21/00	125.89
004	John	Smith	003	003	11/15/99	1597.99
004	John	Smith	004	004	11/22/99	180.92
004	John	Smith	004	005	12/15/99	565.00
004	John	Smith	006	006	10/8/99	25.00
004	John	Smith	006	006	10/8/99	25.00
004	John	Smith	006	008	12/29/99	109.12
006	John	Jones	002	001	10/10/99	250.65
006	John	Jones	002	002	2/21/00	125.89
006	John	Jones	003	003	11/15/99	1597.99
006	John	Jones	004	004	11/22/99	180.92
006	John	Jones	004	005	12/15/99	565.00
006	John	Jones	006	006	10/8/99	25.00
006	John	Jones	006	006	10/8/99	25.00
006	John	Jones	006	008	12/29/99	109.12

Figure 4-8: The PRODUCT of the customers and orders tables

joined_table

ID number (Customers)	first name	last name	ID number (Orders)	order number	order date	order total
001	Jane	Doe	002	001	10/10/99	250.65
001	Jane	Doe	002	002	2/21/00	125.89
001	Jane	Doe	003	003	11/15/99	1597.99
001	Jane	Doe	004	004	11/22/99	180.92
001	Jane	Doe	004	005	12/15/99	565.00
001	Jane	Doe	006	006	10/8/99	25.00
001	Jane	Doe	006	007	11/12/99	85.00
001	Jane	Doe	006	008	12/29/99	109.12
002	John	Doe	002	001	10/10/99	250.65
002	John	Doe	002	002	2/21/00	125.89
002	John	Doe	003	003	11/15/99	1597.99
002	John	Doe	004	004	11/22/99	180.92
002	John	Doe	004	005	12/15/99	565.00
002	John	Doe	006	006	10/8/99	25.00
002	John	Doe	006	007	11/12/99	85.00
002	John	Doe	006	008	12/29/99	109.12
003	Jane	Smith	002	001	10/10/99	250.65
003	Jane	Smith	002	002	2/21/00	125.89
003	Jane	Smith	003	003	11/15/99	1597.99
003	Jane	Smith	004	004	11/22/99	180.92
003	Jane	Smith	004	005	12/15/99	565.00
003	Jane	Smith	006	006	10/8/99	25.00
003	Jane	Smith	006	007	11/12/99	85.00
003	Jane	Smith	006	008	12/29/99	109.12
004	John	Smith	002	001	10/10/99	250.65
004	John	Smith	002	002	2/21/00	125.89
004	John	Smith	003	003	11/15/99	1597.99
004	John	Smith	004	004	11/22/99	180.92
004	John	Smith	004	005	12/15/99	565.00
004	John	Smith	006	006	10/8/99	25.00
004	John	Smith	006	006	10/8/99	25.00
004	John	Smith	006	008	12/29/99	109.12
006	John	Jones	002	001	10/10/99	250.65
006	John	Jones	002	002	2/21/00	125.89
006	John	Jones	003	003	11/15/99	1597.99
006	John	Jones	004	004	11/22/99	180.92
006	John	Jones	004	005	12/15/99	565.00
006	John	Jones	006	006	10/8/99	25.00
006	John	Jones	006	006	10/8/99	25.00
006	John	Jones	006	008	12/29/99	109.12

Figure 4-9: The PRODUCT of the Customers and Orders tables after applying a RESTRICT predicate

The Bottom Line

Because of the processing overhead created when performing a join, some database designers make a conscious decision to leave tables unnormalized. For example, if Lasers Only always accessed the line items at the same time it accessed order information, then a designer might choose to combine the line item and order data into one table, knowing full well that the unnormalized relation exhibits anomalies. The benefit is that retrieval of order information will be faster than if it were split into two tables.

Should you leave unnormalized relations in your database to achieve better retrieval performance? In this author's opinion, there is rarely any need to do so. Assuming that you are working with a relatively standard DBMS that supports SQL as its query language, there are SQL syntaxes that you can use when writing queries that avoid joins. That being the case, it does not seem worth the problems that unnormalized relations present to leave them in the database. Careful writing of retrieval queries can provide performance that is nearly as good as that of retrieval from unnormalized relations.

> *Note: For a complete discussion of writing SQL queries to avoid joins, see the author's book SQL Clearly Explained, also published by AP Professional.*

5

Database Structure and Performance Tuning

For the most part, a DBMS takes care of storing and retrieving data based on a user's commands. The strategy used to process a data manipulation request is handled by the DBMS's *query optimizer*, a portion of the program that determines the most efficient sequence of relational algebra operations to perform a query. You can, however, influence the behavior of the query optimizer and also optimize database performance to some extent with database design elements. In this chapter you will be introduced to three such techniques: indexing, clustering, and partitioning.

Indexing

Indexing is a way of providing a fast access path to the values in a column or a concatenation of columns. New rows are typically added to the bottom of a table, resulting in a relatively random ordering of the values in any given column. Without some way of ordering the data, the only way a DBMS can search a column is by sequentially scanning each row from top to bottom. The larger a table becomes, the slower a sequential search will be.

The conceptual operation of an index is diagrammed in Figure 5-1. (The different weights of the lines have no significance other than to make it easier for you to follow the crossed lines.) In this illustration, you are looking at Lasers Only's merchandise item relation and an index that provides fast access to rows in the table based on the item's title. The index itself contains an ordered list of keys (the titles) along with the locations of the associated rows in the merchandise item table. The rows in the merchandise item table are in relatively random order. However, because the index is in alphabetical order by title, it can be searched quickly to locate a specific title. Then the DBMS can use the information in the index to go directly to a correct row or rows in the merchandise item table, thus avoiding a slow sequential scan of the base table's rows.

Once you have created an index, the DBMS's query optimizer will use the index whenever it determines that using the index will speed up data retrieval. You never need to access the index again yourself unless you want to delete it.

When you create a primary key for a table, the DBMS automatically creates an index for that table using the primary key column or columns as the index key. The first step in inserting a new row into a table is therefore verification that the index key (the primary key of the table) is unique to the index. In fact, uniqueness is enforced by requiring the index entries to be unique, rather than by actually searching the base table. This is much faster than attempting to verify uniqueness directly on the base table because the ordered index can be searched much more rapidly than the unordered base table.

Index **Merchandise item table**

Figure 5-1: Indexing

Deciding Which Indexes to Create

You have no choice as to whether the DBMS creates indexes for your primary keys; you get them whether you want them or not. In addition, you can create indexes to provide fast access to any column or combination of columns you want. However, before you jump headfirst into creating indexes on every column in every table, there are some trade-offs to consider:

- Indexes take up space in the database. Given that disk space is inexpensive today, this is usually not a major drawback.
- When you insert, modify, or delete data in indexed columns, the DBMS must update the index as well as the base table. This may slow down data modification operations, especially if the tables have a lot of rows.
- Indexes definitely speed up access to data.

The trade-off is therefore generally between update speed and retrieval speed. A good rule of thumb is to create indexes for foreign keys and for other columns that are used frequently in queries that apply logical criteria to data. If you find that update speed is severely affected, you may choose at a later time to delete some of the indexes you created.

Clustering

The slowest part of a DBMS's actions is retrieving data from or writing data to a disk. If you can cut down on the number of times the DBMS must read from or write to a disk, you can speed up overall database performance.

The trick to doing this is understanding that a database must retrieve an entire disk *page* of data at one time. The size of a page varies from one operating system to another—it can be anywhere from 512 bytes to 4K, with 1K being typical on a PC—but data always travel to and from disk in page-sized units. Therefore, if you can get data that are often accessed together stored on the same disk page (or on pages that are physically close together), you can speed up data access. This process is known as *clustering* and is available with many DBMSs (for example, Oracle).

> *Note: The term "clustering" has another meaning in the SQL-92 standard. It refers to a group of catalogs (which in turn are groups of schemas) manipulated by the same DBMS. The use of the term in this section, however, is totally distinct from the SQL-92 meaning.*

In practice, a cluster is designed to keep rows related by matching primary and foreign keys together. To define the cluster, you specify a column or columns on which the DBMS should form the cluster and the tables that should be included. Then, all rows that share the same value of the column or columns on which the cluster is based are stored as physically close together as possible. As a result, the rows in a table may be scattered across several disk pages, but matching primary and foreign keys are usually on the same disk page.

Clustering can significantly speed up join performance. However, just as with indexes, there are some trade-offs to consider when contemplating creating clusters:

♦ Because clustering involves physical placement of data in a file, a table can be clustered on only one column or combination of columns.
♦ Clustering can slow down performance of operations that require a scan of the entire table because clustering may mean that the rows of any given table are scattered throughout many disk pages.
♦ Clustering can slow down inserting data.
♦ Clustering can slow down modifying data in the columns on which clustering is based.

Partitioning

Partitioning is the opposite of clustering: It involves the splitting of large tables into smaller ones so that the DBMS does not need to retrieve as much data at any one time. Consider, for example, what happens to Lasers Only's orders and order lines tables over time. Assuming that the business is reasonably successful, those tables (especially order lines) will become very large. Retrieval of data from those tables will therefore begin to slow down.

There are two ways to partition a table: horizontally and vertically. *Horizontal partitioning* involves splitting the rows of a table between two or more tables with the identical structure. *Vertical partitioning* involves splitting the columns of a table, placing them into two or more tables linked by the table's primary key. As you might expect, there are benefits and drawbacks to both.

Horizontal Partitioning

Horizontal partitioning involves creating two or more tables with exactly the same structure and splitting rows between those tables.

Lasers Only might use this technique, for example, to solve problems with the orders and line items tables becoming increasingly large. The database design might be modified as follows:

```
open orders (order number, customer number, order date)
open order lines (order number, item number, quantity, shipped?)
filled orders (order number, customer number, order date)
filled order lines (order number, item number, quantity, shipped?)
```

Whenever all items in an open order have shipped, an application program deletes rows from the open orders and open order lines tables and inserts them into the filled orders and filled order lines tables. The open order and open order lines tables remain relatively small, speeding up both retrieval and modification performance. Although retrieval from filled orders and filled order lines will be slower, Lasers Only uses those tables much less frequently.

The drawback to this solution occurs when Lasers Only needs to access all of the orders and/or order lines at the same time. A query whose result table includes data from both sets of open and filled tables must actually be two queries connected by the UNION operator. Performance of such a query will be worse than that of a query of either set of tables individually. Nonetheless, if an analysis of Lasers Only's data access patterns reveals that such queries occur rarely and that most retrieval involves the open set of tables, then the horizontal partitioning is worth doing.

The only way you can determine whether horizontal partitioning will increase performance is to examine the ways in which your database applications access data. If there is a group of rows that are accessed together significantly more frequently than the rest of the rows in a table, then horizontal partitioning may make sense.

Vertical Partitioning

Vertical partitioning involves creating two or more tables with selected columns and all rows of a table. For example, if Lasers Only

accesses the titles and prices of their merchandise items more frequently than the other columns in the merchandise item table, the
merchandise item table might be partitioned as follows:

```
item titles (item number, title, price)
item details (item number, distributor, release date, …)
```

The benefit of this design is that the rows in the smaller item titles
table will be physically closer together; the smaller table will take
up fewer disk pages and thus support faster retrieval.

Queries that require data from both item tables must join the tables
over the item number. Like most joins, this will be a relatively slow
operation. Therefore, vertical partitioning makes sense only when
there is a highly skewed access pattern for the columns of a table.
The more often a small, specific group of columns is accessed together, the more vertical partitioning will help.

6

Codd's Rules

In October, 1985, E. F. Codd published a series of two articles in the computer industry weekly called *Computerworld*. The first article laid out 12 criteria to which a "fully relational" database should adhere. The second article compared current mainframe products to those 12 rules, producing a flurry of controversy over whether it was important that DBMSs be theoretically rigorous or that they simply work effectively.

To help you understand the issues raised and why Codd's rules for relational databases for the most part make sense, in this chapter we will look at those criteria along with the implications of their implementation. Should you then choose not to adhere to one or more of the rules, you will be doing so with full understanding of the consequences. (In some cases, the consequences are minimal; in others they may significantly affect the integrity of the data in a database.)

Note: The complete citation for Codd's original articles can be found in the bibliography at the end of Chapter 3.

Rule 1: The Information Rule

The first criterion for relational databases deals with the data structures that are used to store data and represent data relationships:

> "All information in a relational database is represented explicitly at the logical level in exactly one way — by values in tables."

The purpose of this rule is to require that relations (two-dimensional tables) be the *only* data structure used in a relational database. Therefore, products that require hard-coded links between tables are not relational.

At the time Codd's article was published, one of the most widely used mainframe products was IDMS/R, a version of IDMS that placed a relational-style query language on top of a simple network database. The simple network data model requires data structures such as pointers or indexes to represent data relationships. Therefore, IDMS/R, although being marketed as relational, was not relational according to the very first rule of a relational database. It was this product that was at the heart of the "who cares about rules if my product works" controversy.

Regardless of which side you take in this particular argument, there are two very good reasons why creating a database from nothing but tables is a good idea:

♦ Logical relationships are very flexible. In a simple network or hierarchical database, the only relationships that can be used for retrieval are those that have been predetermined by the database designer who wrote the schema. However, because a relational database represents its relationships through matching data values, the join operation can be used to implement relations on the fly, even those that a database designer may not have anticipated.

♦ Relational database schemas are very flexible. You can add, modify, and remove individual relations without disturbing the rest of the schema. In fact, as long as you are not changing the structure of tables currently being used, you can modify the schema of a live database. However, to modify the schema of a simple network or hierarchical database you must stop all processing of the database and regenerate the entire schema. In many cases, modifying the database design also means recreating all the physical files (using a dump and load process) to correspond to the new design.

Rule 2: The Guaranteed Access Rule

Given that the entire reason we put data into a database is to get the data out again, we must be certain that we can retrieve every single piece of data:

> "Each and every datum (atomic value) in a relational database is guaranteed to be logically accessible by resorting to a combination of table name, primary key value and column name."

This rule states that you should need to know only three things to locate a specific piece of data: the name of the table, the name of the column, and the primary key of the row.

There is no rule in this set of 12 rules that specifically states that each row in a relation must have a unique primary key. However, a relation cannot adhere to the guaranteed access rule unless it does have unique primary keys. Without unique primary keys, you will retrieve some row with the primary key value used in a search, but not necessarily the exact row you want. Some data may therefore be inaccessible without the ability to uniquely identify rows.

Early relational databases did not require primary keys at all. You could create and use tables without primary key constraints. Today, however, SQL will allow you to create a table without a primary key specification, but most DBMSs will not permit you to enter data into that table.

Rule 3: Systematic Treatment of Null Values

As you know, null is a special database value that means "unknown." Its presence in a database brings special problems during data retrieval. Consider, for example, what happens if you have an employees relation that contains a column for salary. Assume that the salary is null for some portion of the rows. What, then, should happen if someone queries the table for all people who make more than 60,000? Should the rows with null be retrieved or should they be left out?

When the DBMS evaluates a null against the logical criterion of salary value greater than 60,000, it cannot state whether the row containing the null meets the criteria. Maybe it does; maybe it does not. For this reason, we say that relational databases use *three-valued logic*. The result of the evaluation of a logical expression is either true, false, or maybe.

Codd's third rule deals with the issue of nulls:

> "Null values (distinct from the empty character string or a string of blank characters or any other number) are supported in the fully relational DBMS for representing missing information in a systematic way, independent of data type."

First, a relational DBMS must store the same value of null in all columns and rows where the user does not explicitly enter data values. The value used for null must be the same, regardless of the data type of the column. Note that null is not the same as a space character; it has its own, distinct ASCII or UNICODE value. However, in most cases when you see a query's result table on the screen, nulls do appear as blank.

Second, the DBMS must have some consistent, known way of handling those nulls when performing queries. Typically, you will find that rows with nulls are not retrieved by a query such as the salary greater than 60,000 example unless the user explicitly asks for rows with a value of null. Most relational DBMSs today adhere to a three-valued logic truth table to determine retrieval behavior when they encounter nulls.

The inclusion of nulls in a relation can be extremely important. They provide a consistent way to distinguish between valid data such as a 0 and missing data. For example, it makes a great deal of difference to know that the balance in an account payable is 0 instead of unknown. The account with 0 is something we like to see; the account with an unknown balance could be a significant problem.

Rule 4: Dynamic Online Catalog Based on the Relational Model

Earlier in this book you read about relational database data dictionaries. Codd very clearly specifies that those dictionaries (which he calls *catalogs*) should be made up of nothing but relations:

> "The data base description is represented at the logical level in the same way as ordinary data, so that authorized users can apply the same relational language to its interrogation as they apply to regular data."

One advantage of using the same data structures for the data dictionary as you do for data tables is that you have a consistent way to access all elements of the database. You need to learn only one query language. This also simplifies the DBMS itself, since it can use the same mechanism for handling data about the database (*metadata*) as it can data about the organization.

When you purchase a DBMS, it comes with its own way of handling a data dictionary. There is rarely anything you can do to change it. Therefore, the major implication of this particular rule comes in selecting relational software: You want to look for something that has a data dictionary that is made up of nothing but tables.

Rule 5: The Comprehensive Data Sublanguage Rule

A relational database must have some language that can maintain database structural elements, modify data, and retrieve data. Codd included the following rule that describes his ideas about what such a language should do:

"A relational system may support several languages and various modes of terminal use (for example, fill-in-the-blanks mode). However, there must be at least one language whose statements are expressible, per some well-defined syntax, as character strings and that is comprehensive in supporting <u>all</u> of the following items:

- ♦ Data definition
- ♦ View definition
- ♦ Data manipulation (interactive and by program)
- ♦ Integrity constraints
- ♦ Transaction boundaries (begin, commit and rollback)"

The SQL-92 language does meet all of these rules. (Earlier versions did not include complete support for primary keys and referential integrity.) Given that most of today's relational DBMSs use SQL as their primary data manipulation language, there would seem to be no issue here.

However, a DBMS that does not support SQL, but uses a graphic language, would technically not meet this rule. Nonetheless, there are several products today whose graphic language can perform all the tasks Codd has listed without a command-line syntax. Such DBMSs might not be theoretically "fully relational," but since they can perform all the necessary relational tasks, you lose nothing by not having the command-line language.

> *Note: Keep in mind the time frame in which Codd was writing. In 1985, the Macintosh —whose operating system legitimized the graphic user interface — was barely a year old. Most people still considered the GUI-equipped computers to be little more than toys.*

Rule 6: The View Updating Rule

As you will read in more depth in Chapter 7, some views can be used to update data. Others—those that are created from more than one base table or view, those that do not contain the primary keys of their base tables, and so on—cannot be used for updating. Codd's sixth rule speaks only about those that meet the criteria for updatability:

"All views that are theoretically updatable are also updatable by the system."

This rule simply means that if a view meets the criteria for updatability, a DBMS must be able to handle that update and propagate the updates back to the base tables.

Rule 7: High-Level Insert, Update, and Delete

Codd wanted to ensure that a DBMS could handle multiple rows of data at a time, especially when data were modified. Therefore, the seventh rule insists that a DBMS's data manipulation language be able to insert, update, and delete more than one row with a single command:

> "The capability of handling a base relation or a derived relation as a single operand applies not only to the retrieval of data but also to the insertion, update and deletion of data."

SQL provides this capability for today's relational DBMSs. What does it bring you? Being able to modify more than one row with a single command simplifies data manipulation logic. Rather than needing to scan a relation row by row to locate rows for modification, for example, you can specify logical criteria that identify rows to be affected and let the DBMS find the rows for you.

Rule 8: Physical Data Independence

One of the benefits of using a database system rather than a file processing system is that a DBMS isolates the user from physical storage details. The physical data independence rule speaks to that issue:

> "Applications programs and terminal activities remain logically unimpaired whenever any changes are made in either storage representation or access methods."

This means you should be able to move the database from one disk volume to another, change the physical layout of the files, and so on, without any impact on the way in which application programs and end users interact with the tables in the database.

Most of today's DBMSs give you little control over the file structures used to store data on disk. (Only the very largest mainframe systems allow systems programmers to determine physical storage structures.) Therefore, in a practical sense, physical data independence means that you should be able to move the database from one disk volume or directory to another without affecting application programs or interactive users. With few a exceptions—in particular, end-user DBMSs based on the xBase model—most of today's DBMSs do provide physical data independence.

Rule 9: Logical Data Independence

Logical data independence is a bit more subtle than physical data independence. In essence, it means that if you change the schema— perhaps adding or removing a table or adding a column to a table —then other parts of the schema that should not be affected by the change remain unaffected:

> "Application programs and terminal activities remain logical- ly unimpaired when information-preserving changes of any kind that theoretically permit unimpairment are made to the base tables."

As an example, consider what happens when you add a table to a database. Since relations are logically independent of one another, adding a table should have absolutely no impact on any other table. To adhere to the logical data independence rule, a DBMS must en- sure that there is indeed no impact on other tables.

On the other hand, if you delete a table from the database, such a modification is not "information-preserving." Data will almost cer- tainly be lost when the table is removed. Therefore, it is not neces- sary that application programs and interactive users be unaffected by the change.

Rule 10: Integrity Independence

Although the requirement for unique primary keys is a corollary to an earlier rule, the requirement for nonnull primary keys and for referential integrity is very explicit:

"Integrity constraints specific to a particular relational data base must be definable in the relational data sublanguage and storable in the catalog, not in the application programs.

"A minimum of the following two integrity constraints must be supported:

"1. Entity integrity: No component of a primary key is allowed to have a null value.

"2. Referential integrity: For each distinct nonnull foreign key value in a relational data base, there must exist a matching primary key value from the same domain."

Notice that this rule requires that the declaration of integrity constraints must be a part of whatever language is used to define database structure. In addition, integrity constraints of any kind must be stored in a data dictionary that can be accessed while the database is being used.

When IBM released its flagship relational database — DB2 — one of the two things users complained about was the lack of referential integrity support. IBM, and other DBMS vendors for that matter, omitted referential integrity because it slows down performance. Each time you modify a row of data, the DBMS must go to the data dictionary, search for an integrity rule, and perform the test indicated by the rule, all before performing an update. A referential integrity check of a single column can involve two or more disk accesses, all of which takes more time than simply making the modification directly to the base table.

However, without referential integrity, the relationships in a relational database very quickly become inconsistent. Retrieval queries therefore do not necessarily retrieve all data because missing cross-references cause joins to omit data. In that case, the database is unreliable and virtually unusable. (Yes, IBM added referential integrity to DB2 fairly quickly!)

Note: One solution to the problem of a DBMS not supporting referential integrity was to have application programmers perform the referential integrity checks within application programs. This certainly works, but it puts the burden of integrity checking in the wrong place. It should be an integral part of the database, rather than left up to an application programmer.

Rule 11: Distribution Independence

A distributed database is a database where the data themselves are stored on more than one computer. The database is therefore the union of all its parts. In practice, the parts are not unique but contain a great deal of duplicated data.

Nonetheless, according to rule 11:

"A relational DBMS has distribution independence."

In other words, a distributed database must look to the user like a centralized database. Application programs and interactive users should not be required to know where data are stored, including the location of multiple copies of the same data.

DBMS vendors have been working on distributed DBMS software since the late 1970s. However, at the time this book was written, no relational DBMS truly met this rule. Even the most sophisticated distributed DBMS software requires that the user indicate some location information when retrieving data.

Rule 12: Nonsubversion Rule

The final rule might be subtitled the "no cheating rule":

"If a relational system has a low-level (single-record-at-a-time) language, that low-level language cannot be used to

subvert or bypass the integrity rules or constraints expressed in the higher level relational language (multiple-
records-at-a-time)."

Many DBMS products during the 1980s had languages that could
directly access rows in tables, separate from SQL, which operates
on multiple rows at a time. This rule states that there must be no
way to use that direct-access language to get around the integrity
constraints stored in the data dictionary. The integrity rules must be
observed without exceptions.

Part Two

Practice

In this part of the book you will read about some of the practical techniques we use when working with relational database designs. You will be introduced to the SQL language statements needed to create relational schemas and their contents. You will also see how a CASE tool can help design and document a database. In addition, this part contains two complete relational design case studies to provide further examples of the database design process.

7

Using SQL to Implement a Relational Design

As a complete data manipulation language, SQL contains statements that allow you to insert, modify, delete, and retrieve data. However, to a database designer, the portions of SQL that support the creation of database structural elements are of utmost importance. In this chapter you will be introduced to the SQL commands that you will use to create and maintain the tables, views, indexes, and other structures that make up a relational database.

The actual file structure of a database is implementation dependent, as is the procedure needed to create database files. Therefore, the discussion in this chapter assumes that the necessary database files are already in place.

Database Object Hierarchy

The objects in a database maintained by a SQL-92–compliant DBS are arranged in a hierarchy, diagrammed in Figure 7-1. The smallest units with which are database works—the columns and rows—appear in the center. These in turn are grouped into tables and views.

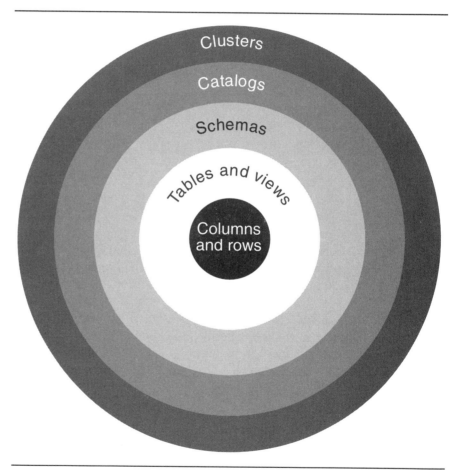

Figure 7-1:   The SQL-92 database object hierarchy

The tables and views that comprise a single logical database are collected into a schema. Multiple schemas are grouped into catalogs, which can then be grouped into clusters. A catalog usually contains information describing all the schemas handled by one DBMS. Catalog creation is implementation dependent and therefore not part of the SQL-92 standard.

Prior to SQL-92, clusters often represented database files, and the clustering of objects into files was a way to increase database performance by placing objects accessed together in the same physical file. The SQL-92 concept of a cluster, however, is a group of catalogs that are accessible using the same connection to a database server.

Under SQL-92, none of the groupings of database objects are related to physical storage structures. If you are working with a centralized mainframe DBMS, you may find multiple catalogs stored in the database file. However, on smaller or distributed systems, you are just as likely to find one catalog or schema per database file or to find a catalog or schema split between multiple files.

Clusters, catalogs, and schemas are not required elements of a database environment. In a small installation where there is one collection of tables serving a single purpose, for example, it may not even be necessary to create a schema to hold them.

Naming and Identifying Objects

The way in which you name and identify database objects is in some measure dictated by the object hierarchy:

- Column names must be unique within the table.
- Table names must be unique within the schema.
- Schema names must be unique within their catalog.
- Catalog names must be unique within their cluster.

When a column name appears in more than one table in a query, a user must specify the table from which a column should be taken (even if it makes no difference which table is used). The general form for qualifying duplicate names is:

```
table_name.column_name
```

If an installation has more than one schema, then a user must also indicate the schema in which a table resides:

`schema_name.table_name.column_name`

This naming convention means that two different schemas can include tables with the same name.

By the same token, if an installation has multiple catalogs, a user will need to indicate the catalog from which an object comes:

`catalog_name.schema_name.table_name.column_name`

The names that you assign to database elements can include the following:

- ◆ Letters
- ◆ Numbers
- ◆ Underscores (_)

Names can be up to 128 characters long. They are not case-sensitive. (In fact, many SQL command processors convert names to all upper- or lowercase characters before submitting a SQL statement to a DBMS for processing.)

Note: Some DBMSs also allow pound signs (#) and dollar signs ($) in element names, but neither is recognized by SQL queries so their use should be avoided.

Schemas

To a database designer, a schema represents the overall, logical design of a complete database. As far as SQL is concerned, however, a schema is nothing more than a container for tables, views, and other structural elements. It is up to the database designer to place a meaningful group of elements within each schema.

A schema is not required to create tables and views. In fact, if you are installing a database for an environment in which there is likely to be only one logical database, then you can just as easily do without one. However, if more than one database will be sharing the same DBMS and the same server, then organizing database elements into schemas can greatly simplify the maintenance of the individual databases.

Creating a Schema

To create a schema, you use the CREATE SCHEMA statement. In its simplest form, it has the syntax

```
CREATE SCHEMA schema_name
```

as in

```
CREATE SCHEMA lasers_only
```

By default, a schema belongs to the user who created it (the user ID under which the schema was created). The owner of the schema is the only user ID that can modify the schema unless the owner grants that ability to other users.

To assign a different owner to a schema, you add an AUTHORIZATION clause:

```
CREATE SCHEMA schema_name AUTHORIZATION owner_user_ID
```

For example, to assign the lasers_only schema to the user ID DBA, someone could use:

```
CREATE SCHEMA lasers_only AUTHORIZATION dba
```

When creating a schema, you can also create additional database elements at the same time. To do so, you use braces to group the CREATE statements for the other elements, as in:

```
CREATE SCHEMA schema_name AUTHORIZATION owner_user_ID
{
    other create statements go here
}
```

This automatically assigns the elements within the braces to the schema.

Identifying the Schema You Want to Use

One of the nicest things about a relational database is that you can add or delete database structure elements at any time. There must therefore be a way to specify a current schema for new database elements after the schema has been created initially with the CREATE SCHEMA statement.

One way to do this is with the SET SCHEMA statement:

```
SET SCHEMA schema_name
```

To use SET SCHEMA, the user ID under which you are working must have authorization to work with that schema.

Alternatively, you can qualify the name of a database element with the name of the schema. For example, if you are creating a table, then you would use something like

```
CREATE TABLE schema_name.table_name
```

For those DBMSs that do not support SET SCHEMA, this is the only way to attach new database elements to a schema after the schema has been created.

Domains

As you know, a domain is an expression of the permitted values for a column in a relation. When you define a table, you assign each column a data type (for example, character or integer) that provides a broad domain. A DBMS will not store data that violate that constraint.

The SQL-92 standard introduced the concept of user-defined domains, which can be viewed as user-defined data types that can be applied to columns in tables. (This means you have to create a domain before you can assign it to a column!)

Domains can be created as part of a CREATE SCHEMA statement or, if your DBMS supports SET SCHEMA, at any time after a schema has been defined.

To create a domain, you use the CREATE DOMAIN statement, which has the following general syntax:

```
CREATE DOMAIN domain_name data_type
CHECK (expression_to_validate_values)
```

The CHECK clause is actually a generic way of expressing a condition that data must meet. It can include a SELECT to validate data against other data stored in the database or it can include a simple logical expression. In that expression, the keyword VALUE represents the data being checked.

For example, if Lasers Only wanted to validate the price of a disc, someone might create the following domain:

```
CREATE DOMAIN price numeric (6,2)
CHECK (VALUE >= 19.95)
```

After creating this domain, a column in a table can be given the data type of price. The DBMS will then check to be certain that the value in that column is always greater than or equal to 19.95. (We will leave a discussion of the data type used in the preceding SQL statement until we cover creating tables in the next section of this chapter.)

The domain mechanism is very flexible. Assume, for example, that you want to ensure that telephone numbers are always stored in the format XXX-XXX-XXXX. A domain to validate that format might be created as:

```
CREATE DOMAIN telephone char (12)
CHECK (SUBSTRING (VALUE FROM 4 FOR 1 = '-') AND
    SUBSTRING (VALUE FROM 8 FOR 1 = '-'))
```

You can use the CREATE DOMAIN statement to give a column a default value. For example, the following statement sets up a domain that holds either Y or N and defaults to Y:

```
CREATE DOMAIN boolean char (1)
DEFAULT 'Y'
CHECK (UPPER(VALUE) = 'Y' OR UPPER(VALUE) = 'N')
```

Tables

The most important structure within a relational database is the table. As you know, tables contain just about everything, including business data and the data dictionary.

The SQL-92 standard divides tables into three categories:

- ♦ Permanent base tables: Permanent base tables are tables whose contents are stored in the database and remain permamently in the database unless they are explicitly deleted.
- ♦ Global temporary tables: Global temporary tables are tables used for working storage that are destroyed at the end of a SQL session. The definitions of the tables are stored in the data dictionary, but their data are not. The tables must be loaded with data each time they are going to be used. Global temporary tables can be used only by the current user, but they are visible to an entire SQL session (either an application program or a user working with an interactive query facility).
- ♦ Local temporary tables: Local temporary tables are similar to global temporary tables. However, they are visible only to the specific program module in which they are created.

Temporary base tables are subtly different from views, which assemble their data by executing a SQL query. You will read more about this difference and how temporary tables are created and used later in this chapter.

Most of the tables in a relational database are permanent base tables. You create them with the CREATE TABLE statement:

```
CREATE TABLE table_name
(   column1_name column1_data_type
    column_constraints,
    column2_name column2_data_type
    column_constraints, …
    table_constraints)
```

The constraints on a table include declarations of primary and foreign keys. The constraints on a column include whether values in the column are mandatory as well as other constraints you may decide to include in a CHECK clause.

Column Data Types

Each column in a table must be given a data type. Although data types are somewhat implementation dependent, you can expect to find most of the following:

- ♦ INTEGER (abbreviated INT): A positive or negative whole number. The number of bits occupied by the value is implementation dependent. On today's desktop computers, an integer is either 16 or 32 bits. Large computers use only 32-bit integers.
- ♦ SMALLINT: A positive or negative whole number. A small integer is usually half the size of a standard integer. Using small integers when you know you will need to store only small values can save space in the database.
- ♦ NUMERIC: A fixed-point positive or negative number. A numeric value has a whole number portion and a fractional portion. When you create it, you must specify the total length of the number (including the decimal point) and how many of those digits will be to the right of the decimal point (its precision). For example:

```
NUMERIC (6,2)
```

creates a number in the format XXX.XX. The DBMS will store exactly two digits to the right of the decimal point.

- DECIMAL: A fixed-point positive or negative number. A decimal number is similar to a numeric value. However, the DBMS may store more digits to the right of the decimal than you specify. Although there is no guarantee that you will get the extra precision, its presence can provide more accurate results in computations.
- REAL: A "single-precision" floating point value. A floating point number is expressed in the format:

```
±X.XXXXX * 10YY
```

where YY is the power to which 10 is raised. Because of the way in which computers store floating point numbers, a real number will never be an exact representation of a value, but only a close approximation. The range of values that can be stored is implementation dependent, as is the precision. You therefore cannot specify a size for a real number column.
- DOUBLE PRECISION (abbreviated DOUBLE): A "double-precision" floating point number. The range and precision of double precision values are implementation dependent, but generally both will be greater than with single-precision real numbers.
- FLOAT: A floating point number for which you can specify the precision. The DBMS will maintain at least the precision that you specify. (It may be more.)
- BIT: Storage for a fixed number of individual bits. You must indicate the number of bits, as in

```
BIT (n)
```

where n is the number of bits. (If you do not, you will have room for only one bit.)
- BIT VARYING: Storage for a varying number of bits, up to a specified maximum, as in

```
BIT VARYING (n)
```

where n is the maximum number of bits. In some DBMSs, columns of this type can be used to store graphic images.
- DATE: A date.

- ◆ TIME: A time.
- ◆ TIMESTAMP: The combination of a date and a time.
- ◆ CHARACTER (abbreviated CHAR): A fixed-length space to hold a string of characters. When declaring a CHAR column, you need to indicate the width of the column:

```
CHAR (n)
```

where n is the amount of space that will be allocated for the column in every row. Even if you store less than n characters, the column will always take up n bytes and the column will be padded with blanks to fill up empty space. The maximum number of characters allowed is implementation dependent.

- ◆ CHARACTER VARYING (abbreviated VARCHAR): A variable length space to hold a string of characters. You must indicate the maximum width of the column—

```
VARCHAR (n)
```

—but the DBMS stores only as many characters as you insert, up to the maximum n. The overall maximum number of characters allowed is implementation dependent.

- ◆ INTERVAL: A date or time interval. An interval data type is followed by a qualifier that specifies the size of the interval and optionally the number of digits. For example:

```
INTERVAL YEAR
INTERVAL YEAR (n)
INTERVAL MONTH
INTERVAL MONTH (n)
INTERVAL YEAR TO MONTH
INTERVAL YEAR (n) TO MONTH
INTERVAL DAY
INTERVAL DAY (n)
INTERVAL DAY TO HOUR
INTERVAL DAY (n) TO HOUR
INTERVAL DAY TO MINUTE
INTERVAL DAY (n) TO MINUTE
INTERVAL MINUTE
INTERVAL MINUTE (n)
```

In the preceding examples, n specifies the number of digits. When the interval covers more than one date–time unit, such as YEAR TO MONTH, you can specify a size for only the first unit. Year–month intervals can include years, months, or both. Time intervals can include days, hours, minutes, and/or seconds.

Notice that there is no specification for a Boolean (true–false) data type. This means that if you need to use a column as a flag, the best solution is to create a boolean domain like the one you saw earlier in this chapter in the section on domains.

In Figure 7-2 you will find bare-bones CREATE TABLE statements for the Lasers Only database. These statements include only column names and data types. SQL will create tables from statements in this format, but because the tables have no primary keys, many DBMSs will not let you enter data.

Default Values

As you are defining columns, you can designate a default value for individual columns. To indicate a default value, you add a DEFAULT keyword to the column definition, followed by the default value. For example, in the Orders relation the order_date column defaults to the current system date. The column declaration is therefore written:

```
order_date date DEFAULT CURRENT_DATE
```

Notice that this particular declaration is using the SQL value CURRENT_DATE. However, you can place any value after DEFAULT that is a valid instance of the column's data type.

NOT NULL Constraints

The values in primary key columns must be unique and not null. In addition, there may be columns for which you want to require a

```
CREATE TABLE customer
    (customer_numb int,
    customer_first_name varchar (15),
    customer_last_name varchar (15),
    customer_street varchar (30),
    customer_city varchar (15),
    customer_state char (2),
    customer_zip char (5),
    customer_phone char (12),
    credit_card_numb varchar (15),
    card_exp_date date)

CREATE TABLE item
    (item_numb integer,
    title varchar (60),
    distributor_numb int,
    retail_price numeric (6,2),
    release_date date,
    genre char (15))

CREATE TABLE order
    (order_numb integer,
    customer_numb integer,
    order_date date,
    order_filled char (1))

CREATE TABLE order_line
    (order_numb int,
    item_numb int,
    quantity integer,
    discount_applied numeric (6,2),
    selling_price numeric (6,2),
    shipped char (1))

CREATE TABLE distributor
    (distributor_numb int,
    distributor_name varchar (15),
    distributor_street varchar (30),
    distributor_city varchar (15),
    distributor_state char (2),
    distributor_zip char (5),
    distributor_phone char (12),
    distributor_contact_person varchar (30),
    contact_person_ext varchar (5))
```

Continued next page

Figure 7-2: Initial CREATE TABLE statements for the Lasers Only database

```
CREATE TABLE actor
    (actor_numb int,
    actor_name varchar (30)

CREATE TABLE performance
    {actor_numb int,
    item_numb int,
    role varchar (30))

CREATE TABLE producer
    (producer_name varchar (30),
    studio varchar (30))

CREATE TABLE production
    (producer_name varchar (30),
    item_numb int)
```

Figure 7-2: (Continued)   Initial CREATE TABLE statements for the Lasers Only database

value. You can specify such columns by adding NOT NULL after the column declaration. Since the online bookstore wants to ensure that an order date is always entered, the complete declaration for that column in the Orders table is:

```
order_date date NOT NULL DEFAULT CURRENT_DATE
```

Primary Keys

To specify a table's primary key, you add a PRIMARY KEY clause to a CREATE TABLE statement. The keywords PRIMARY KEY are followed by the names of the primary key column or columns, surrounded by parentheses.

In Figure 7-3 you will find the CREATE TABLE statements for the Lasers Only database including primary key declarations. Notice that in the order_lines, performance, and production tables, all of which which have a concatenated primary key, both primary key columns have been included in the PRIMARY KEY clause.

```
CREATE TABLE customer
    (customer_numb int,
    customer_first_name varchar (15),
    customer_last_name varchar (15),
    customer_street varchar (30),
    customer_city varchar (15),
    customer_state char (2),
    customer_zip char (5),
    customer_phone char (12) NOT NULL,
    credit_card_numb varchar (15),
    card_exp_date date
    PRIMARY KEY (customer_numb))

CREATE TABLE item
    (item_numb integer,
    title varchar (60),
    distributor_numb int,
    retail_price numeric (6,2),
    release_date date,
    genre char (15)
    PRIMARY KEY (item_numb))

CREATE TABLE order
    (order_numb integer,
    customer_numb integer,
    order_date date,
    order_filled char (1)
    PRIMARY KEY (order_numb)

CREATE TABLE order_line
    (order_numb int,
    item_numb int,
    quantity integer,
    discount_applied numeric (6,2),
    selling_price numeric (6,2),
    shipped char (1)
    PRIMARY KEY (order_numb, item_numb))
```

Continued next page

Figure 7-3:   CREATE TABLE statements for the Lasers Only database including primary key declarations

```
CREATE TABLE distributor
    (distributor_numb int,
    distributor_name varchar (15),
    distributor_street varchar (30),
    distributor_city varchar (15),
    distributor_state char (2),
    distributor_zip char (5),
    distributor_phone char (12),
    distributor_contact_person varchar (30),
    contact_person_ext varchar (5)
    PRIMARY KEY distributor_numb)

CREATE TABLE actor
    (actor_numb int,
    actor_name varchar (30)
    PRIMARY KEY (actor_numb))

CREATE TABLE performance
    {actor_numb int,
    item_numb int,
    role varchar (30)
    PRIMARY KEY actor_numb, item_numb))

CREATE TABLE producer
    (producer_name varchar (30),
    studio varchar (30)
    PRIMARY KEY (producer_name))

CREATE TABLE production
    (producer_name varchar (30),
    item_numb int)
    PRIMARY KEY (producer_name, item_numb))
```

Figure 7-3: (Continued)   CREATE TABLE statements for the Lasers Only database including primary key declarations

Foreign Keys

As you know, a foreign key is a column (or concatenation of columns) that is exactly the same as the primary key of some table. When a foreign key value matches a primary key value, we know that there is a logical relationship between the database objects represented by the matching rows.

One of the major constraints on a relation is referential integrity, which states that every nonnull foreign key value must reference an existing primary key value. To maintain the integrity of the database, it is vital that foreign key constraints be stored within the database's data dictionary so that the DBMS can be responsible for enforcing those constraints.

To specify a foreign key for a table, you add a FOREIGN KEY clause:

```
FOREIGN KEY foreign_key_name (foreign_key_columns)
REFERENCES primary_key_table (primary_key_columns)
ON UPDATE update_action
ON DELETE delete_action
```

The names of the foreign key columns follow the keywords FOREIGN KEY. The REFERENCES clause contains the name of the primary key table being referenced. If the primary key columns are named in the PRIMARY KEY clause of their table, then you don't need to list the column names. However, if the columns aren't part of a PRIMARY KEY clause, you must list the primary key columns in the REFERENCES clause.

The final part of the FOREIGN KEY specification indicates what should happen when a primary key value being referenced by the foreign key is deleted or updated. There are three options that apply to both updates and deletions and one additional option for each:

- SET NULL: Replace the foreign key value with null. This isn't possible when the foreign key is part of the primary key of its table.
- SET DEFAULT: Replace the foreign key value with the column's default value.
- CASCADE: Delete or update all foreign key rows.
- NO ACTION: On update, make no modification of foreign key values.
- RESTRICT: Do not allow deletion of the primary key row.

The complete declarations for the Lasers Only database tables, which includes foreign key constraints, can be found in Figure 7-4. Notice that although there are no restrictions on how to name foreign keys, the foreign keys in this database have been named to indicate the tables involved. This makes them easier to identify if you need to delete or modify a foreign key at a later date.

Additional Column Constraints

There are additional constraints that you can place on columns in a table beyond primary and foreign key constraints. These include requiring unique values and predicates in CHECK clauses.

Requiring Unique Values

If you want to ensure that the values in a non–primary key column are unique, then you can use the UNIQUE keyword. UNIQUE verifies that all nonnull values are unique. For example, if you were storing social security numbers in an employees table that used an employee ID as the primary key, you could also enforce unique social security numbers with:

```
ssn char (11) UNIQUE
```

The UNIQUE clause can also be placed at the end of the CREATE TABLE statement, along with the primary key and foreign key specifications. In that case, it takes the form:

```
UNIQUE (column_names)
```

Check Clauses

The CHECK clause to which you were introduced earlier in this chapter in the Domains section can also be used with individual columns to declare column-specific constraints. To add a constraint, you place a CHECK clause after the column declaration, using the keyword VALUE in a predicate to indicate the value being checked.

For example, to verify that a column used to hold true–false values is limited to T and F, you could write a CHECK clause as:

```
CHECK (UPPER(VALUE) = 'T' OR UPPER(VALUE) = 'F')
```

```
CREATE TABLE customer
    (customer_numb int,
    customer_first_name varchar (15),
    customer_last_name varchar (15),
    customer_street varchar (30),
    customer_city varchar (15),
    customer_state char (2),
    customer_zip char (5),
    customer_phone char (12) NOT NULL,
    credit_card_numb varchar (15),
    card_exp_date date
    PRIMARY KEY (customer_numb))

CREATE TABLE item
    (item_numb integer,
    title varchar (60),
    distributor_numb int,
    retail_price numeric (6,2),
    release_date date,
    genre char (15)
    PRIMARY KEY (item_numb)
    FOREIGN KEY (item2distributor)
    REFERENCES distributor (distributor_numb)
        ON UPDATE CASCADE
        ON DELETE RESTRICT)

CREATE TABLE order
    (order_numb integer,
    customer_numb integer,
    order_date date,
    order_filled char (1)
    PRIMARY KEY (order_numb)
    FOREIGN KEY (order2customer)
    REFERENCES customer (customer_numb)
        ON UPDATE CASCADE
        ON DELETE RESTRICT)

CREATE TABLE actor
    (actor_numb int,
    actor_name varchar (30)
    PRIMARY KEY (actor_numb))
```

Continued next page

Figure 7-4:   Complete CREATE TABLE statements for the Lasers Only
database including primary and foreign key declarations

```
CREATE TABLE order_line
    (order_numb int,
    item_numb int,
    quantity integer,
    discount_applied numeric (6,2),
    selling_price numeric (6,2),
    shipped char (1)
    PRIMARY KEY (order_numb, item_numb)
    FOREIGN KEY (order_line2order)
    REFERENCES order (order_numb)
        ON UPDATE CASCADE
        ON DELETE RESTRICT
    FOREIGN KEY (order_line2item)
    REFERENCES item (item_numb)
        ON UPDATE CASCADE
        ON DELETE RESTRICT)

CREATE TABLE performance
    {actor_numb int,
    item_numb int,
    role varchar (30)
    PRIMARY KEY actor_numb, item_numb)
    FOREIGN KEY (performance2actor)
    REFERENCES actor (actor_numb)
        ON UPDATE CASCADE
        ON DELETE CASCADE
    FOREIGN KEY (performance2item)
    REFERENCES item (item_numb)
        ON UPDATE CASCADE
        ON DELETE CASCADE)

CREATE TABLE producer
    (producer_name varchar (30),
    studio varchar (30)
    PRIMARY KEY (producer_name))

CREATE TABLE production
    (producer_name varchar (30),
    item_numb int)
    PRIMARY KEY (producer_name, item_numb)
    FOREIGN KEY (production2producer)
    REFERENCES producer (producer_name)
        ON UPDATE CASCADE
        ON DELETE CASCADE
    FOREIGN KEY (production2item)
    REFERENCES item (item_numb)
        ON UPDATE CASCADE
        ON DELETE CASCADE)
```

Figure 7-4: (Continued)   Complete CREATE TABLE statements for the Lasers Only database including primary and foreign key declarations

Views

As you first read in Chapter 3, views provide a way to give users a specific portion of a larger schema with which they can work. Before you actually can create views, there are two things you should consider: which views you really need and whether the views can be used for updating data.

Deciding Which Views to Create

Views take up very little space in a database, occupying only a few rows in a data dictionary table. That being the case, you can feel free to create views as needed.

A typical database might include the following views:

- ◆ One view for every base table that is exactly the same as the base table, but with a different name. Then, you prevent end users from seeing the base tables and do not tell the end users the table names; you give end users access only to the views. This makes it harder for end users to attempt to gain access to the stored tables because they do not know their names. However, as you will see in the next section, it is essential for updating that there be views that do match the base tables.
- ◆ One view for each primary key–foreign key relationship over which you join frequently. If the tables are large, the actualy syntax of the query may include methods for avoiding the join operation but still combining the tables.
- ◆ One view for each complex query that you issue frequently.
- ◆ Views as needed to restrict user access to specific columns and rows. For example, you might recreate a view for a receptionist that shows employee office numbers and telephone extensions, but leaves off home address, telephone number, and salary.

View Updatability Issues

A database query can apply any operations supported by the DBMS's query language to a view, just as it can to base tables. However, using views for updates is a much more complicated issue. Given that views exist only in main memory, any updates made to a view must be stored in the underlying base tables if the updates are to have any effect on the database.

Not every view is updatable, however. Although the rules for view updatability vary from one DBMS to another, you will find that most DBMSs share the following restrictions:

♦ A view must be created from no more than one base table or view.
♦ If the source of the view is another view, then the source view must also adhere to the rules for updatability.
♦ A view must be created from only one query. Two or more queries cannot be assembled into a single view table using operations such as union.
♦ The view must include the primary key columns of the base table.
♦ The view must include all columns specified as not null (columns requiring mandatory values).
♦ The view must not include any groups of data. It must include the original rows of data from the base table, rather than rows based on values common to groups of data.
♦ The view must not remove duplicate rows.

Creating Views

To create a view whose columns have the same name as the columns in the base tables from which it is derived, you give the view a name and include the SQL query that defines its contents:

```
CREATE VIEW view_name AS
    SELECT …
```

For example, if Lasers Only wanted to create a view that included action films, the SQL is written:

```
CREATE VIEW action AS
    SELECT title_numb, title
    FROM item
    WHERE genre = 'action'
```

If you want to rename the columns in the view, you include the new column names in the CREATE VIEW statement:

```
CREATE VIEW action
    (identifier, name)
AS
    SELECT title_numb, title
    FROM item
    WHERE genre = 'action'
```

The preceding statement will produce a view with two columns named Identifier and Name. Note that if you want to change even one column name, you must include *all* the column names in the parentheses following the view name. The DBMS will match the columns following SELECT with the view column names by their position in the list.

Views can be created from any SQL query, including those that perform joins, unions, and grouping. For example, to simplify looking at sales figures, Lasers Only might create a view like the following:

```
CREATE VIEW sales_summary AS
    SELECT customer_numb, orders.order_numb, orders.order_date,
        SUM (selling_price)
    FROM order_line JOIN order
    GROUP BY customer_numb, orders.order_date, orders.order_numb
```

The view table will then contain grouped data along with a computed column.

Temporary Tables

A temporary table is a base table that is not stored in the database but instead exists only while the database session in which it was created is active. At first glance, this may sound like a view, but views and temporary tables are rather different:

+ A view exists only for a single query. Each time you use the name of a view, its table is recreated from existing data.
+ A temporary table exists for the entire database session in which it was created.
+ A view is automatically populated with the data retrieved by the query that defines it.
+ You must add data to a temporary table with SQL INSERT commands.
+ Only views that meet the criteria for view updatability can be used for data modification.
+ Because temporary tables are base tables, all of them can be updated.
+ Because the contents of a view are generated each time the view's name is used, a view's data are always current.
+ The data in a temporary table reflect the state of the database at the time the table was loaded with data. If the data from which the temporary table was loaded are modified after the temporary table has received its data, then the contents of the temporary table may be out of sync with other parts of the database.

If the contents of a temporary table become outdated when source data change, why use a temporary table at all? Wouldn't it be better simply to use a view whose contents are continually regenerated? The answer lies in performance. It takes processing time to create a view table. If you are going to use data only once during a database session, then a view will actually perform better than a temporary table because you don't need to create a structure for it. However, if you are going to be using the data repeatedly during a session, then a temporary table provides better performance because it needs to be created only once. The decision therefore results in a trade-off: Using a view repeatedly takes more time but provides continually updated data; using a temporary table repeatedly saves time, but you run the risk that the table's contents may be out of date.

Creating Temporary Tables

Creating a temporary table is very similar to creating a permanent base table. You do, however, need to decide on the *scope* of the table. A temporary table can be *global*, in which case it is accessible to the entire application program that created it. Alternatively, it can be *local*, in which case it is accessible only to the program module in which it was created.

To create a global temporary table, you add the keywords **GLOBAL TEMPORARY** to the **CREATE TABLE** statement:

```
CREATE GLOBAL TEMPORARY TABLE
    ( remainder of CREATE statement)
```

By the same token, you create a local temporary table with:

```
CREATE LOCAL TEMPORARY TABLE
    (remainder of CREATE statement)
```

For example, if Lasers Only was going to use the sales summary information repeatedly, it might create the following temporary table instead of using a view:

```
CREATE GLOBAL TEMPORARY TABLE sales_summary
(customer_numb INTEGER,
order_numb INTEGER,
order_date DATE,
order_total NUMERIC (6,2),
PRIMARY KEY (customer_numb,order_numb))
```

Loading Temporary Tables with Data

To place data in a temporary table, you use one or more SQL IN-
SERT statements. For example, to load the Sales_summary table
created in the preceding section, you could write:

```
INSERT INTO sales_summary
   SELECT customer_numb, orders.order_numb, orders.order_date,
      SUM (selling_price)
   FROM order_line JOIN order
   GROUP BY customer_numb, orders.order_date, orders.order_numb
```

You can now query and manipulate the `Sales_summary` table just
as you would a permanent base table.

Disposition of Temporary Table Rows

When you write embedded SQL, you have control over the amount
of work that the DBMS considers to be a unit (a *transaction*). To understand what happened to the rows in a temporary table, you do
need to know that a transaction can end in one of two ways: It can
be *committed* (its changes made permanent) or it can be *rolled back*
(its changes undone).

By default, the rows in a temporary table are purged whenever a
transaction is committed. You can, however, instruct the DBMS to
retain the rows by including **ON COMMIT PRESERVE ROWS** to the
end of the table creation statement:

```
CREATE GLOBAL TEMPORARY TABLE sales_summary
(customer_numb INTEGER,
order_numb INTEGER,
order_date DATE,
order_total NUMERIC (6,2),
PRIMARY KEY (customer_numb,order_numb),
ON COMMIT PRESERVE ROWS)
```

Because a rollback returns the database to the state it was in before
the transaction began, a temporary table will also be restored to its
previous state (with or without rows).

Creating Indexes

As you read in Chapter 5, an index is a data structure that provides a fast access path to rows in a table based on the values in one or more columns (the index key). Because an index stores key values in order, the DBMS can use a fast search technique to find the values rather than being forced to search each row in an unordered table sequentially.

You create indexes with the **CREATE INDEX** statement:

```
CREATE INDEX index_name
ON table_name (index_key_columns)
```

For example, to create an index on the title column in the Item table, the online bookstore would use:

```
CREATE INDEX title
ON item (title)
```

By default, the index will allow duplicate entries and sorts the entries in ascending order. To require unique index entries, add the keyword UNIQUE after CREATE:

```
CREATE UNIQUE INDEX title
ON item (title)
```

To sort in descending order, insert DESC after the column whose sort order you want to change. For example, Lasers Only might want to create an index on order_date in the Order relation in descending order so that the most recent orders are first:

```
CREATE INDEX order_date
ON order (order_date DESC)
```

If you want to create an index on a concatenated key, you include all the columns that should be part of the index key in the column list. For example, the following creates an index organized by actor and item number:

```
CREATE INDEX actor_item
ON performance (actor_numb, item_numb)
```

Although you do not need to access an index directly unless you want to delete it from the database, it helps to give indexes names that tell you something about their keys. This makes it easier to re-member them should you need to get rid of the indexes.

Modifying Database Elements

With the exception of tables, database elements are largely un-changeable. When you want to modify them, you must delete them from the database and create them from scratch. In contrast, just about every characteristic of a table can be modified without delet-ing the table using the ALTER TABLE statement.

Adding New Columns

To add a new column to a table, you use the ALTER TABLE state-ment with the following syntax:

```
ALTER TABLE table_name
ADD column_name column_data_type column_constraints
```

For example, if Lasers Only wanted to add a telephone number col-umn to the Producer table they would use:

```
ALTER TABLE producer
ADD phone CHAR (12)
```

To add more than one column at the same time, simply separate the clauses with commas:

```
ALTER TABLE producer
ADD phone CHAR (12),
ADD producer_street VARCHAR (30),
ADD producer_city VARCHAR (30),
ADD producer_state CHAR (2),
ADD producer_zip CHAR (5)
```

Adding Table Constraints

You can add table constraints such as foreign keys at any time. To do so, include the new constraint in the ADD clause of an ALTER TABLE statement:

```
ALTER TABLE table_name
ADD table_constraint
```

Assume, for example, that Lasers Only created a new table named States and included in it all the two-character U.S. state abbreviations. The company would then need to add references to that table from the Customer, Distributor, and Producer tables:

```
ALTER TABLE customer
ADD FOREIGN KEY customers2states (customer_state)
    REFERENCES states (state_name)

ALTER TABLE distributor
ADD FOREIGN KEY distributor2states (distributor_state)
    REFERENCES states (state_name)

ALTER TABLE publisher
ADD FOREIGN KEY publishers2states (publisher_state)
    REFERENCES states (state_name)
```

When you add a foreign key constraint to a table, the DBMS verifies that all existing data in the table meet that constraint. If they do not, the ALTER TABLE will fail.

Modifying Columns

You can modify columns by changing any characteristic of the column, including its data type, size, and constraints:

♦ To replace a complete column definition, use the MODIFY command with the current column name and the new column characteristics. For example, to change the customer number in the Customer table from an integer to a character column, the online bookstore could use:

```
ALTER TABLE customers
MODIFY customer_numb CHAR (4)
```

♦ To add or change a default value only (without changing the data type or size of the column), include the DE-FAULT keyword:

```
ALTER TABLE customers
MODIFY customer_numb DEFAULT 0
```

♦ To switch between allowing nulls and not allowing nulls without changing any other column characteristics, add NULL or NOT NULL as appropriate:

```
ALTER TABLE customers
MODIFY customer_zip NOT NULL
```

or

```
ALTER TABLE customers
MODIFY customer_phone NULL
```

♦ To modify a column constraint without changing any other column characteristics, include a CHECK clause:

```
ALTER TABLE item
MODIFY retail_price
    CHECK (VALUE >= 19.95)
```

When you change the data type of a column, the DBMS will attempt to convert any existing values to the new data type. If the current values cannot be converted, then the table modification will not be performed. In general, most columns can be converted to character. However, conversions from a character data type to numbers or datetimes require that existing data represent legal values in the new data type.

Deleting Elements

You can also delete structural elements from a table as needed:

♦ To delete a column:

```
ALTER TABLE order_line
DELETE line_cost
```

♦ To delete a CHECK table constraint (a CHECK that has been applied to an entire table rather than to a specific column):

```
ALTER TABLE customer
DELETE CHECK
```

♦ To remove the UNIQUE constraint from one or more columns:

```
ALTER TABLE item
DELETE UNIQUE (title)
```

♦ To remove a table's PRIMARY KEY:

```
ALTER TABLE customer
DELETE PRIMARY KEY
```

Although you can delete a table's primary key, keep in mind that if you do not add a new one, you will not be able to modify any data in that table.

♦ To delete a foreign key:

```
ALTER TABLE item
DELETE FOREIGN KEY item2distributor
```

Renaming Elements

You can rename both tables and columns:

♦ To rename a table, place the new table name after the RENAME keyword:

```
ALTER TABLE order_line
RENAME line_item
```

♦ To rename a column, include both the old and new column names separated by the keyword TO:

```
ALTER TABLE item
RENAME title TO item_title
```

Deleting Database Elements

To delete a structural element from a database, you *drop* the element. For example, to delete a table, you would type:

```
DROP TABLE table_name
```

Dropping a table is irreversible. In most cases, the DBMS will not bother to ask you "are you sure?" but will immediately delete the structure of the table and all of its data.

You can remove the following elements from a database with the DROP statement:

- Tables
- Views

```
DROP VIEW view_name
```

- Indexes

```
DROP INDEX index_name
```

- Domains

```
DROP DOMAIN domain_name
```

A DROP of a table or view will fail if the element being dropped is currently in use by another user.

Granting and Revoking Access Rights

When you create an element of database structure, the user name under which you are working becomes that element's owner. The owner has the right to do anything to that element; all other users have no rights at all. This means that if tables and views are going to be accessible to other users, you must *grant* them access rights.

Types of Access Rights

There are six types of access rights that you can grant:

- ♦ SELECT: Allows a user to retrieve data from a table or view.
- ♦ INSERT: Allows a user to insert new rows into a table or updatable view. Permission may be granted to specific columns rather than the entire database element.
- ♦ UPDATE: Allows a user to modify rows in a table or updatable view. Permission may be granted to specific columns rather than the entire database element.
- ♦ DELETE: Allows a user to delete rows from a table or updatable view.
- ♦ REFERENCES: Allows a user to reference a table as a foreign key in a table he or she creates. Permission may be granted to specific columns rather than the entire table.
- ♦ ALL PRIVILEGES: Gives a user all of the preceding rights to a table or view.

By default, granting access rights to another user does not give that user the right to pass on those rights to others. If, however, you add a WITH GRANT OPTION clause, you give the user the ability to grant the rights that he or she has to another user.

Storing Access Rights

Access rights to tables and views are stored in the data dictionary. Although the details of the data dictionary tables vary from one DBMS to another, you will usually find access rights split between two system tables named something like Systableperm and Syscolperm. The first table is used when access rights are granted to entire tables or views; the second is used when rights are granted to specific columns within a table or view.

A Systableperm table has a structure similar to the following:

```
systableperm (table_id, grantee, grantor, selectauth, insertauth,
    deleteauth, updateauth, updatecols, referenceauth)
```

The columns represent:

- table_id: An identifier for the table or view.
- grantee: The user ID to which rights have been granted.
- grantor: The user ID granting the rights.
- selectauth: The grantee's SELECT rights.
- insertauth: The grantee's INSERT rights.
- deleteauth: The grantee's DELETE rights.
- updateauth: The grantee's UPDATE rights.
- updatecols: Indicates whether rights have been granted to specific columns within the table or view. When this value is Y (yes), the DBMS must also look in Syscolperm to determine whether a user has the rights to perform a specific action against the database.
- referenceauth: The grantee's REFERENCE rights.

The columns that hold the access rights take one of three values: Y (yes), N (no), or G (Yes with grant option).

Whenever a user makes a request to the DBMS to manipulate data, the DBMS first consults the data dictionary to determine whether the user has the rights to perform the requested action. If the DBMS cannot find a row with a matching user ID and table identifier, then the user has no rights at all to the table or view. If a row with a matching user ID and table identifier exist, then the DBMS checks for the specific rights that the user has to the table or view and—based on the presence of Y, N, or G in the appropriate column—either permits or disallows the requested database access.

Granting Rights

To grant rights to another user, a user that either created the database element (and therefore has all rights to it) or has GRANT rights issues a GRANT statement:

```
GRANT type_of_rights
ON table_or_view_name TO user_ID
```

For example, if the DBA of Lasers Only wants to allow the accounting manager (who has a user ID of acctg_mgr) to access the sales summary view, the DBA would type:

```
GRANT SELECT
ON sales_summary TO acctg_mgr
```

To allow the accounting manager to pass those rights on to other users, the DBA would need to add one line to the SQL;

```
GRANT SELECT
ON sales_summary TO acctg_mgr
WITH GRANT OPTION
```

If Lasers Only wants to give some student interns limited rights to some of the base tables, the GRANT might be written:

```
GRANT SELECT, UPDATE (retail_price, distributor_numb)
ON item TO intern1, intern2, intern3
```

The preceding example grants SELECT rights to the entire table but gives UPDATE rights only on two specific columns. Notice also that you can grant multiple rights in the same command as well as give the same group of rights to more than one user. However, a single GRANT applies to only one table or view.

In most cases, rights are granted to specific user IDs. You can, however, make database elements accessible to anyone by granting rights to the special user ID PUBLIC. For example, the following statement gives every authorized user the rights to see the sales_summary view:

```
GRANT SELECT
ON sales_summary TO PUBLIC
```

Revoking Rights

To remove previously granted rights, you use the REVOKE statement, whose syntax is almost the opposite of GRANT:

```
REVOKE access_rights
FROM table_or_view_name FROM user_ID
```

For example, if Lasers Only's summer interns have finished their work, the DBA might want to remove their access from the database:

```
REVOKE SELECT, UPDATE (retail_price, distributor_numb)
ON item FROM intern1, intern2, intern3
```

If the user from which you are revoking rights has the GRANT option for those rights, then you also need to make a decision about what to do if the user has passed on those rights. In the following case, the REVOKE will be disallowed if the acctg_mgr user has passed on his or her rights:

```
REVOKE SELECT
ON sales_summary FROM acctg_mgr
RESTICT
```

In contrast, the syntax

```
REVOKE SELECT
ON sales_summary FROM acctg_mgr
CASCADE
```

will remove the rights from the acctg_mgr ID along with any user IDs to which acctg_mgr granted rights.

8

Using CASE Tools for Database Design

A CASE (computer-aided software engineering) tool is a software package that provides support for the design and implementation of information systems. By integrating many of the techniques used to document a system design—including the data dictionary, data flows, and entity relationships—CASE software can increase the consistency and accuracy of a database design.

> *Note: It is also true that CASE tools can save you a lot of time when it comes to drawing ER diagrams. At a guess, the complete Lasers Only ER diagram would have taken about 10 hours to draw using a graphics package but only about 2 hours using a CASE tool.*

There are many CASE tools on the market. The diagrams and screens you will see throughout this chapter come from MacA&D.

Although the exact "look" of the diagrams is specific to this one particular package, the software capabilities you will see are typical of most CASE tools.

A word of warning is in order about CASE tools before we proceed any further: A CASE tool is exactly that—a tool. It can document a database design and it can provide invaluable help in maintaining the consistency of a design. However, it cannot design the database for you. There is no software in the world that can examine a database environment and identify the entities, attributes, and relationships that should be represented in a database. The model created with CASE software is therefore only as good as the analysis of the database environment performed by the people using the tool.

CASE Capabilities

Most CASE tools organize the documents pertaining to a single system into a "project." As you can see in Figure 8-1, by default a typical project supports the following types of documents:

- ♦ Data dictionary: In most CASE tools, the data dictionary forms the backbone of the project, providing a single repository for all processes, entities, attributes, and domains used anywhere throughout the project.
- ♦ Requirements: Requirements are usually text specifications of what individual parts of the system must do.
- ♦ Data flow diagrams: As you read in Chapter 2, data flow diagrams document the way in which data travel throughout an organization, indicating who handles the data. Although it isn't necessary to create data flow diagrams if your only goal with the project is to document a database design, data flow diagrams can often be useful in documenting the relationships between multiple organization units and the data they handle. Data flow diagrams can, for example, help you determine whether an organization needs a single database or a combination of databases.

Figure 8-1:   CASE software project documents

- ◆ Structure charts: Structure charts are used to model the structure of application programs that will be developed using structured programming techniques. The charts show the relationship between program modules.
- ◆ Data models: Data models are the ER diagrams that you have been reading about.
- ◆ Screen prototypes: Drawings of sample screen layouts are typically most useful for documenting the user interface of application programs. However, they can also act as a cross-check to ensure that a database design is complete by allowing you to verify that everything needed to generate the sample screen designs is present in the database.
- ◆ State models: State models, documented in state transition diagrams, indicate the ways in which data change.
- ◆ Task diagrams: Task diagrams are used to help plan application programs in which multiple operations (tasks) must occur at the same time. They are therefore not particularly relevant to the database design process.

♦ Class diagrams: Class diagrams are used when performing object-oriented rather than structured analysis.
♦ Object diagrams: Object diagrams are used during object-oriented analysis to indicate how objects communicate with one another by passing messages.

Although object-oriented analysis can be used as the launching point for a relational database, it is better suited to the object-oriented data model and therefore will not be discussed in this book.

Many of the diagrams and reports that a CASE tool can provide are designed to follow a single theoretical model. For example, the ER diagrams that you have seen earlier in this book might be based on the Chen model or the Information Engineering model. Any given CASE tool will support some selection of diagramming models. You must therefore examine what a particular product supports before you purchase it to ensure that it provides exactly what you need.

ER Diagram Reports

In addition to providing tools for simplifying the creation of ER diagrams, many CASE tools can generate reports that document the contents of an ERD. For example, in Figure 8-2 you can see a portion of a report that provides a description of each entity and its attributes, including the attribute's data type. For many designers, this type of report actually constitutes a paper-based data dictionary.

A CASE tool can also translate the relationships in an ER diagram into a report such as that in Figure 8-3. The text in the report describes the cardinality of each relationship in the ERD and can therefore be very useful for pinpointing errors that may have crept into the graphic version of the diagram.

```
ENTITY SPECIFICATION
DIAGRAMS IN DOCUMENT: Lasers Only

Entity: actor

Attributes:

...*actor_numb
DataType: INT

...actor_name
DataType: CHAR (40)


Entity: customer

Attributes:

...*customer_numb: int
DataType: INT

...customer_first_name: char (15)
DataType: CHAR (15)

...customer_last_name: char (15)
DataType: CHAR (15)

...customer_street: char (25)
DataType: CHAR (30)

...customer_city: char (15)
DataType: CHAR (30)

...customer_state: char (2)
DataType: CHAR (2)

...customer_zip: char (10)
DataType: CHAR (10)

...customer_phone: char (12)
DataType: CHAR (12)

...credit_card_numb: char (20)
DataType: CHAR (30)

...card_exp_date: date
DataType: DATE
```

Figure 8-2:   Part of an entity specifications report

```
RELATION SPECIFICATION
DIAGRAMS IN DOCUMENT: Lasers Only

customer is associated with zero or more instances of order.
order is associated with one and only one instance of customer.

distributors is associated with zero or more instances of items.
items is associated with one and only one instance of distributors.

order is associated with zero or more instances of order_lines.
order_lines is associated with one and only one instance of order.

items is associated with zero or more instances of order_lines.
order_lines is associated with one and only one instance of items.

actor is associated with zero or more instances of performance.
performance is associated with one and only one instance of actor.

items is associated with zero or more instances of performance.
performance is associated with one and only one instance of items.

producer is associated with zero or more instances of production.
production is associated with one and only one instance of
producer.

items is associated with zero or more instances of production.
production is associated with one and only one instance of items.
```

Figure 8-3:   A relation specification report

Data Flow Diagrams

There are two widely used styles for data flow diagrams: Yourdon/ DeMarco (which has been used throughout this book) and Gane & Sarson.

The Yourdon/Demarco style, which you can see in Figure 8-4, uses circles for processes. (This particular example is for a small taxi company that rents its cabs to drivers.) Data stores are represented by parallel lines. Data flows are curved or straight lines with labels that indicate the data that are moving along that pathway. External sources of data are represented by rectangles.

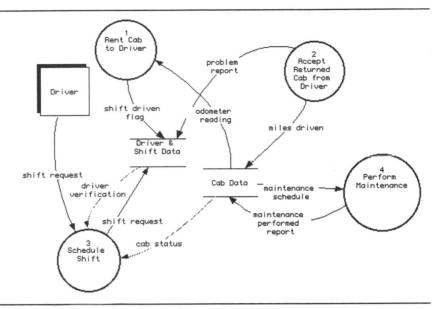

Figure 8-4:   Yourdon/DeMarco style DFD

In concept, the Gane & Sarson style is very similar; it varies primarily in style. As you can see in Figure 8-5, the processes are round-cornered rectangles as opposed to circles. Data stores are open-ended rectangles rather than parallel lines. External sources of data remain as rectangles and data flows use only straight lines. However, the concepts of numbering the processes and exploding each process with a child diagram that shows further detail is the same, regardless of which diagramming style you use.

As mentioned earlier, DFDs are very useful in the database design process for helping a designer to determine whether an organization needs a single, integrated database or a collection of independent databases. For example, it is clear from the taxi company's DFDs that an integrated database is required. Of the four processes shown in the diagram, three use data from both the cab data store and the driver and shift data store. (Only the maintenance process uses just one data store.) You will see further examples of using DFDs in this way throughout the case studies in the rest of this book.

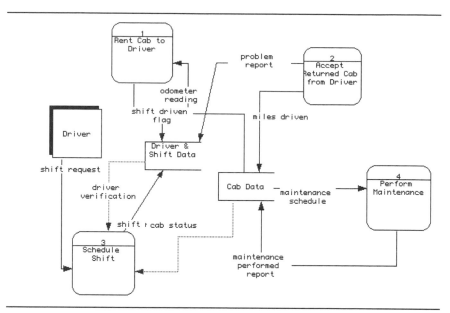

Figure 8-5:   Gane & Sarson style DFD

The Data Dictionary

From a database designer's point of view, the ER diagram and its associated data dictionary are the two most important parts of CASE software. Since you were introduced to several types of ER diagrams in Chapter 2, we will not repeat them here but instead focus on the interaction of the diagrams and the data dictionary.

A data dictionary provides a central repository for documenting entities, attributes, and domains. In addition, by linking entries in the ER diagram to the data dictionary, you can provide enough information for the CASE tool to generate the SQL CREATE statements needed to define the structure of the database.

The layout of a data dictionary varies with the specific CASE tool, as does the way in which entries are configured. With Mac A&D, for example, all attributes, entities, and domains appear in a single alpahbetical list (see Figure 8-6). Domain names begin with a $, but there is no simple way when first viewing the dictionary to distinguish between entities and attributes.

Figure 8-6:   A data dictionary window

However, if you double-click on an item, then its declaration appears in the dictionary window, as in Figure 8-7. Double-clicking on an entity displays the domain that has been assigned (see Figure 8-8).

As you look at the data dictionary, keep in mind that a data dictionary is not intended to show the actual design of a database. Many of the attributes listed in the data dictionary are used by more than one table. Maintaining a hierarchy of attributes and tables would therefore require duplicating data dictionary entries for each table in which an attribute appeared. Instead, a data dictionary typically provides an alphabetical list of elements in which you can look up the definition of an element, regardless of where it is used within

Figure 8-7:   The definition of an entity showing in a data dictionary window

the database. Its purpose is also to ensure that a given database element is defined consistently. For example, wherever the customer number is used in the Lasers Only database, it will be an integer.

Nonetheless, if you need a visual representation of the structure of an entity, most CASE tools will build some sort of tree diagram for you. For example, the diagram in Figure 8-9 shows the stucture of the customer entity.

The linking of data dictionary entries to an ER diagram has one major benefit. Assuming that each attribute has a single entry in the data dictionary, then CASE software can examine an ER diagram and automatically identify foreign keys. This is yet another way in which the consistency of attribute definitions enforced by a CASE tool's data dictionary can support the database design process.

Figure 8-8:   The definition of an attribute showing in a data dictionary window

Figure 8-9:   A tree diagram showing entity structure

Most CASE tools will provide a way for you to store the characteristics of an attribute in the data dictionary. For example, in Figure 8-10, you will find a window used to indicate an attribute's domain and any additional constraints that should be placed on the attribute (in this case, NOT NULL) and to enter a short description of the attribute. Once those details have been saved, they appear as part of the attribute's definition in the data dictionary (Figure 8-11).

Attribute Details

Name: credit_card_numb

Data Type: CHAR (30)   Types

Default:

Constraint:
NOT NULL

Description:
Customer credit card number used as security when renting a disc.

OK   Cancel

Figure 8-10:   Storing attribute details

Code Generation

The end product of most database design efforts is a set of SQL CREATE TABLE commands. If you are using CASE software and the software contains a complete data dictionary, then the software can generate the SQL for you. In most cases, the code will be saved in a text file, which you can then use as input to a DBMS.

The effectiveness of the SQL that a CASE tool can produce, as you might expect, depends on the completeness of the data dictionary entries. To get truly usable SQL, the data dictionary must contain:

Figure 8-11:   A complete attribute definition stored in the data dictionary

- ◆ Domains for every attribute
- ◆ Primary key definitions (created as attributes are added to entities in an ER diagram)
- ◆ Foreign key definitions (created by CASE tool after ER diagram is complete)
- ◆ Any additional constraints that arc to be placed on individual attributes (created when adding attributes to entities in the ER diagram)

Sample Input and Output Designs

As mentioned in the first section of this chapter, sample screen designs are typically of most use to application programmers. However, they can also support the database designer by providing a way to double-check that the database can provide all the data needed by application programs. Most CASE tools therefore provide a way to draw and label sample screen and report layouts.

For example, one of the most important things that the person scheduling cab reservations for the taxi company needs to know is which cabs are not reserved for a given date and shift. A simple screen such as that in Figure 8-12 will do the trick. The diagram shows what data the user needs to enter (the shift date and the shift name). It also shows the output (cab numbers). The names of the fields on the sample screen design can be linked automatically to the data dictionary.

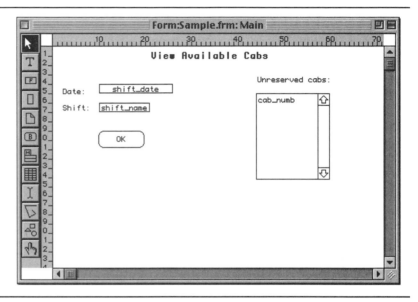

Figure 8-12:   Sample screen design

A CASE tool can be used to model a entire application program. The "browse" tool at the very bottom of the tool bar in Figure 8-12 switches into browse mode, in which buttons and menus become active. Users can make choices from pull-down menus that can be linked to other forms. Buttons can also trigger the opening of other forms. Users can click into data entry fields and tab between fields. Users can therefore not only see the layout of input and output screens and documents but also navigate through an application.

The Drawing Environment

To this point, you've been reading about the way in which the functions provided by CASE software can support the database design effort. In this last section we will briefly examine the tools you can expect to find as part of CASE software, tools with which you can create the types of documents you need.

Because most of the documents you create with CASE software are diagrams, the working environment of a CASE tool is primarily a specialized graphics environment. For example, in Figure 8-13 you can see the drawing tools provided by Mac A&D for creating ER diagrams. (Keep in mind that each CASE tool will differ somewhat in the precise layout of its drawing tool bar, but the basic capabilities will be the same.)

Figure 8-13: Example CASE tool drawing environment for ER diagrams

The important thing to note is that the major shapes needed for the diagrams are provided as individual tools. You therefore simply click on the tool you want to use in the tool bar and draw the shape in the diagram, just as you would if you were working with a general-purpose graphics program.

9

Database Design Case Study #1: Mighty-Mite Motors

It is not unusual for a database designer to be employed to reengineer the information systems of an established corporation. As you will see from the company described in this chapter, information systems in older companies have often grown haphazardly, with almost no planning and integration. The result is a hodgepodge of data repositories that cannot provide the information needed for the corporation to function because they are isolated from one another. In such a situation, it is the job of the database designer to examine the environment as a whole and to focus on the integration of data access across the corporation as well as the design of one or more databases that will meet individual department needs.

On the bright side, an organization such as Mighty-Mite Motors, which has a history of data processing of some kind, knows quite well what it needs in an information system, even if the employees are unable to articulate those needs immediately. There will almost certainly be a collection of paper forms and reports that the organization uses regularly. Such documents specify the input and output needs of the organization and can greatly simplify a database designer's task.

Corporate Overview

Mighty-Mite Motors, Inc. (MMM) is a closely held corporation, established in 1980, that designs, develops, manufactures, and markets miniature ridable motor vehicles for children. Products include several models of cars, trucks, all-terrain vehicles, and trains (see Figure 9-1). Vehicles are powered by car batteries and achieve top speeds of about 5 mph.

At this time, MMM is organized into three divisions: Product Development, Manufacturing, and Marketing & Sales. Each division is headed by a vice president who reports directly to the CEO. (An organization chart appears in Figure 9-2.) All three divisions are housed in a single location that the corporation owns outright.

Product Development Division

The Product Development division is responsible for designing and testing new products. The division employs design engineers who use computer-aided design (CAD) software to prepare initial designs for new vehicles. Once a design is completed, between 1 and 10 prototypes are built. The prototypes are first tested in house using robotic drivers–passengers. After refinement, the prototypes are tested by live children in a variety of settings. Feedback from the testers is used to refine product designs and to make decisions about which designs should actually be manufactured for mass marketing.

Mighty-Mite Motors

Product Catalog

Winter Holiday Season 2001

Figure 9-1: Mighty-Mite Motors product catalog

Model # 001

All Terrain Vehicle: Accelerator in the handlegrip lets young riders reach speeds of up to 5 miles per hour. Vehicle stops immediately when child removes his or her hand from the handlegrip. Can carry one passenger up to 65 lbs. **Suggested retail price: $124.95**

Model #002

4 Wheel Drive Cruiser: Two-pedal drive system lets vehicle move forward at $2\,^{1}/2$ mph on hard surfaces, plus reverse. Electronic speed reduction for beginners. Includes one 6v battery and one recharger. Ages 3–7 (can carry two passengers up to 65 lbs. each). **Suggested retail price: $149.99**

Figure 9-1: (Continued)   Mighty-Mite Motors product catalog

Model # 003

Classic roadster: Sounds include engine start-up, rev, shifting gears, and idle. Two forward speeds— $2\,^1/2$ mph and 5 mph; reverses at $2\,^1/2$ mph. High-speed lockout. On/off power pedal. Power-Lock electric brake. Includes two 6v batteries and recharger. Ages 3–7 (can carry two passengers up to 65 lbs. each). **Suggested retail price: $189.99**.

Model #004

Sports car #1: Two forward speeds, $2\,^1/2$ and 5 mph. Reverses at $2\,^1/2$ mph. High-speed lockout. Power-Lock electric brake. Includes two 6v batteries and one recharger. Ages 3–6 (can carry two passengers up to 90 lbs. combined). **Suggested retail price: $249.99**.

Model #005

Sports car #2: Phone lets child pretend to talk while he or she drives. Two forward speeds—$2\,^1/2$ and 5 mph; reverses at $2\,^1/2$ mph. High-speed lockout. Power-Lock electric brake. Includes two 6v batteries and one recharger. Ages 3–6 (can carry two passengers up to 90 lbs. combined). **Suggested retail price: $249.99**.

Model #006

Turbo Injected Porsche 911: Working stick shift—3 and 6 mph forward; 3 mph reverse. High-speed lockout. Adjustable seat. Doors, trunk, and hood open. Simulated car phone. Includes one 18v battery and recharger. Ages 3–8 (can carry two passengers up to 120 lbs combined). **Suggested retail price: $299.99.**

Model #007

Indy Car: Dual motors for cruising on a variety of surfaces, even up hills. Two forward speeds (2 ^{1}/2 and 5 mph), plus reverse (2 ^{1}/2 mph). Adjustable seat. Includes two 6v batteries and recharger. Ages 3–7 (can carry one passenger up to 80 lbs.). **Suggested retail price: $269.99.**

Model #008

2-Ton Pickup Truck: In metallic teal color. Simulated chrome engine covers and headlight with over-size wheels. 2 ^{1}/2 mph forward speed. Includes one 6v battery and recharger. Ages 3–7 (can carry one passenger up to 65 lbs.). **Suggested retail price: $189.99.**

Figure 9-1: (Continued)   Mighty-Mite Motors product catalog

Model #009

Santa Fe Train: Soundly engineered by a little guy or gal. A hand-operated on/off button controls the 6v battery-operated motor. Reaches speeds to 3 mph. Even includes a battery-powered "whoo whoo" whistle to greet passersby. Rides on 76" x 168" oval track (sold separately) or carpet or sidewalk, indoors or outdoors. Plastic body and floorboard; steel axles and coupling pins. Bright red, blue, and yellow body features a large lift-up seat and trailing car for storage. Includes battery and charger. Ages 3–6. **Suggested retail price: $159.90.**

Model #010

Oval Track: Measures 76" by 168". **Suggested retail price: $39.90.**

Model #011

Additional 6-Pc Straight Track: Six straight sections 19" each (total 105"). **Suggested retail price: $19.90.**

Figure 9-1: (Continued)   Mighty-Mite Motors product catalog

Model #012

Rechargeable Batteries (6 volt): For use with 6 or 12 volt vehicles. For 12 volt vehicles, use two. To charge, use charger included with vehicle. **Suggested retail price: $27.99**.

Figure 9-1: (Continued)   Mighty-Mite Motors product catalog

Figure 9-2:   Mighty-Mite Motors organization chart

Manufacturing Division

The Manufacturing division is responsible for producing products for mass market sales. Manufacturing procures its own raw materials and manages its own operations, including personnel (hiring, firing, scheduling) and assembly line management. Manufacturing maintains the inventory of products ready for sale. It also handles shipping of products to resellers, based on sales information received from Marketing & Sales.

Marketing & Sales Division

MMM sells directly to toy stores and catalog houses; the corporation has never used distributors. Marketing & Sales employs a staff of 25 salespeople who make personal contacts with resellers. Salespeople are responsible for distributing catalogs in their territories, visiting and/or calling potential resellers, and taking reseller orders. Order accounting is handled by Marketing & Sales. As noted earlier, Marketing & Sales transmits shipping information to Manufacturing, which takes care of actual product delivery.

Current Information Systems

MMM's information systems are a hodgepodge of computers and applications that have grown up with little corporate planning. The Product Development division relies primarily on stand-alone CAD workstations. In contrast to the sophistication of the CAD workstations, testing records are kept and analyzed manually. Product Development employs product designers (some of whom function as project leaders) and clerical support staff, but no information systems personnel. Attempts to have clerical staff develop simple database applications to store data about children who test new products and the results of those tests have proved futile. It has become evident that Product Development needs information systems professionals, and although the division is willing to hire IS staff, corporate management has decided to centralize the IS staff, rather than add to a decentralized model.

Manufacturing uses a stand-alone minicomputer to track purchases and inventory levels of raw materials, personnel scheduling, manufacturing line scheduling, and finished product inventory. Each of these applications was written in COBOL in the early 1980s, shortly after the corporation was established. The data used by a Manufacturing application are contained in files that do not share information with any of the other applications. Manufacturing employs a data processing staff of five, most of whom are COBOL maintenance programmers. Although these programmers are talented, the basic applications no longer meet the needs of the Manufacturing division and management has determined that it isn't cost effective to rewrite them from scratch.

Marketing & Sales, which wasn't computerized until 1987, has a local area network consisting of one server and 15 workstations. The server provides shared applications such as word processing and spreadsheets. It also maintains a marketing and sales database, which has been developed using dBase III Plus. The database suffers from several problems, including a limit of 10 users at one time and concurrency control problems that lead to severe data inconsistencies. The marketing and sales database was developed by one member of the division's three-person IS staff. However, that individual left the company in 1992 and no current staff member totally understands the software. Regardless of the amount of time spent trying to maintain the database, inaccurate data continue to be introduced.

The Marketing & Sales LAN has no data communications capabilities. Salespeople therefore must transmit hard copies of their orders to the central office, where the orders are manually keyed into the existing database. (Some of the salespeople do have laptop computers, but because the LAN has no modems, the salespeople cannot connect to it.)

Reengineering Project

Because MMM seems to have lost its strategic advantage in the marketplace, the CEO has decided to undertake a major systems reengineering project. The overall thrust of the project is to provide an integrated information system that will support better evaluation of product testing, better analysis of sales patterns, and better control of the manufacturing process. New information systems will be based on a client–server model and include one or more databases running on a network of servers, workstations, and PCs.

New Information Systems Division

The first step in the reengineering project is to establish an Information Systems division. This new division will also be housed in the corporate headquarters, along with the three existing divisions. To accommodate the new division, MMM will be constructing a 10,000 square foot addition to its building.

MMM is in the process of searching for a Chief Information Officer (CIO). This individual, who will report directly to the CEO, will manage the new division and be responsible for overseeing the reengineering of computer-based information systems that will handle all of the corporation's operations.

All current IS personnel (those who work for the Manufacturing and Marketing & Sales divisions) will be transferred to the new IS division. The division will hire (either internally or externally) three management-level professionals: a Lead Programmer (responsible for overseeing application development), a Database Administrator (responsible for database design and management), and a Lead Analyst (responsible for overseeing systems analysis and design efforts). Retraining in the client–server model and client–server development tools will be provided for all current employees who are willing to make the transition. Those who are unwilling to move to the new development environment will be laid off.

Basic System Goals

The CEO has defined the following goals for the reengineering project:

- ◆ Develop a corporation-wide data administration plan that documents all databases to be developed for the corporation. This documentation will include ER diagrams, schemas, and data dictionaries.
- ◆ Provide an application road map that documents all application programs that will be needed to provide access to corporate databases.

◆ Create a timeline for the installation of corporate databases and the development of application programs.

◆ Specify hardware changes and/or acquisitions that will be necessary to support access to the databases from within the headquarters building and by salespeople who are traveling. Although not every employee will have access to every database, the equipment should nonetheless make universal access possible, providing maximum flexibility for future growth.

◆ Develop and implement a security plan that supports access restrictions to the corporate databases.

◆ Install the databases and develop application programs.

◆ Acquire and install necessary hardware upgrades.

Current Business Processes

To aid the systems analysts in their assessment of MMM's information systems needs, the CEO of MMM asked all existing division heads to document the way in which information is currently processed. This documentation, which also includes some information about what an improved system should do, provides a starting point for the redesign of both business and IS processes.

The Sales and Ordering Processes

MMM receives orders at its plant in two ways: either by telephone directly from customers or from members of the sales staff who have visited customers in person. Orders from the remote sales staff usually arrive by fax or overnight courier.

Each order is taken on a standard order form (Figure 9-3). If the order arrives by fax, it will already be on the correct form. Telephone orders are written directly onto the form. Several times a day a clerk enters the orders into the dBase III database application. Unfortunately, if the sales office is particularly busy, order entry may be delayed. This backup has a major impact on production line scheduling and thus on the company's ability to fill orders. The new information system must streamline the order-entry process, including the electronic transmission of orders from the field and the direct entry of in-house orders into electronic form.

The in-house sales staff has no access to the computer files that show the current finished-goods inventory. They are therefore unable to tell customers when their orders will ship. They can, however, tell customers how many orders are ahead of theirs to be filled and, based on general manufacturing timetables, come up with an approximation of how long it will take to ship a given order. One of the goals of the information systems reengineering project is to provide better company-wide knowledge of how long it will take to fill customer orders.

The Manufacturing, Inventory, and Shipping Processes

The MMM Manufacturing division occupies a large portion of the MMM facility. The division controls the actual manufacturing lines (three assembly lines), a storage area for finished goods, a storage area for raw materials, and several offices for supervisory and clerical staff.

The manufacturing process is triggered when a batch of order forms is received each morning by the manufacturing office. (The batch consists of all orders that were entered into the sales database the previous working day.) A secretary takes the individual order forms and compiles a report summarizing the number ordered by model (Figure 9-4). This report is then given to the Manufacturing Supervisor, whose responsibility it is to schedule which model will be produced on each manufacturing line each day.

The scheduling process is somewhat complex, because the Manufacturing Supervisor must take into account previously placed orders, which have determined the current manufacturing schedule, and current inventory levels as well as the new orders when adjusting the schedule. The availability of raw materials and the time it takes to modify a manufacturing line to produce a different model also enter into the scheduling decision. This is one function that MMM's management understands will be almost impossible to automate; there is too much human expertise involved to translate it

Mighty-Mite Motors

Customer Order Form

Customer #:

Order date:

Name:

Street:

City: State: Zip:

Voice phone #:   Fax:

First name: Contact person   Last name:

Item #	Quantity	Unit Price	Line Total

Order total:

Figure 9-3:   Mighty-Mite Motors order form

Mighty-Mite Motors
Order Summary

mm/dd/yyyy

Model #	Quantity Ordered
001	75
002	150
004	80
005	35
008	115
009	25
010	25
011	15

Figure 9-4: Mighty-Mite Motors order summary report format

into an automatic process. However, it is vital that the Manufacturing Supervisor have access to accurate, up-to-date information about orders, inventory, and the current line schedule so that judgements can be made based on as much hard data as possible.

As finished vehicles come off the assembly line, they are packed for shipping, labeled, and sent to finished goods storage. Each shipping carton contains one vehicle, which is marked with its model number, serial number, and date of manufacturing. The Shipping Manager, who oversees finished goods storage and shipping, ensures that newly manufactured items are entered into the existing inventory files.

The Shipping Manager receives customer order forms after the order report has been completed. (Photocopies of the order forms are kept in the Marketing & Sales office as backup.) The orders are placed in a box in reverse chronological order so that the oldest orders can be filled first. The Shipping Manager checks orders against inventory levels by looking at the inventory level output screen (Figure 9-5). If the manager sees that there is enough inventory to fill an order, then the order is given to a shipping clerk for processing. If there isn't enough inventory, then the order is put back in the box, where it will be checked again the following day. Under this system, no partial orders are filled because they would be extremely difficult to track. (The reengineered information system should allow handling of partial shipments.)

Current Finished Goods Inventory Levels
mm/dd/yy

INV#	NUMBER ON HAND
001	215
002	35
003	180
004	312
005	82
006	5
007	212
008	189
009	37
010	111
011	195
012	22

Figure 9-5:   Mighty-Mite Motors inventory screen layout

Shipping clerks are given orders to fill. They create shipping labels for all vehicles that are part of a shipment. The cartons are labeled and set aside for pickup by UPS. The shipping clerks create UPS manifests (which also serve as packing slips), ensure that the items being shipped are removed from the inventory file, and return the filled orders to the Shipping Manager. The orders are then marked as filled and returned to Marketing & Sales. The reengineered information system should automate the generation of pick-lists, packing slips, and updating of finished-goods inventory.

MMM's raw materials inventory is maintained on a just-in-time basis. The Manufacturing Supervisor checks the line schedule (Figure 9-6) and the current raw materials inventory (Figure 9-7) daily to determine what raw materials need to be ordered. This process relies heavily on the Manufacturing Supervisor's knowledge of which materials are needed for which model vehicle. MMM's CEO is very concerned about this process because the Manufacturing Supervisor, while accurate in scheduling the manufacturing line, is nowhere near as accurate in judging raw materials needs. The result is that occasionally manufacturing must stop because raw materials have run out. The CEO would therefore like to see ordering of raw materials triggered automatically. The new information system should keep track of the raw materials needed to produce each model and, based on the line schedule and a reorder point established for each item, generate orders for items when needed.

Raw materials are taken from inventory each morning as each manufacturing line is being set up for the day's production run. The inventory files are modified immediately after all raw materials have been removed for a given manufacturing line. There is no way to automate the reduction of inventory; however, the new information system should make it easy for nontechnical users to update inventory levels.

The Product Testing and Support Function

MMM's top management makes decisions about which model vehicles to produce based on data from three sources: product testing, customer registrations, and problem reports.

Customer registrations are received on cards packaged with sold vehicles (Figure 9-8). Currently, the registration cards are filed by customer name. However, MMM would also like access to these data by model and serial number to make it easier to notify customers if a recall occurs. Management would also like summaries of the data by model purchased, age of primary user, gender of primary user, and who purchased the vehicle for the child.

Problem reports (Figure 9-9) are taken by customer support representatives who work within the product testing division. These reports include the serial number and model experiencing problems along with the date and type of problem. Currently, the problem descriptions are nonstandard, written in whatever language the customer support representative happens to use. It is therefore difficult

Line Schedule
mm/dd/yy

mm/dd/yy

Line #1: Model 005	100 units
Line #2: Model 007	150 units
Line #3: Model 010	100 units

mm/dd/yy

Line #1: Model 003	200 units
Line #2: Model 005	150 units
Line #3: Model 008	300 units

mm/dd/yy

Line #1: Model 006	150 units
Line #2: Model 008	100 units
Line #3: Model 002	300 units

:
:
:

Total production scheduled:

Model 002	300 units
Model 003	200 units
Model 005	250 units
Model 006	150 units
Model 007	150 units
Model 008	400 units
Model 010	100 units

Figure 9-6: **Mighty-Mite Motors line schedule report format**

to summarize problem reports to get an accurate picture of which models are experiencing design problems that should be corrected. MMM would therefore like to introduce a standardized method for describing problems, probably through a set of problem codes. The result should be regular reports on the problems reported for each model that can be used to help make decisions about which models

```
┌─────────────────────────────────────────────────────────┐
│              Current Raw Materials Inventory Levels       │
│                        mm/dd/yy                           │
│                                                           │
│     ITEM#          ITEM              QUANTITY ON HAND      │
│     001       Plastic #3             95 lbs               │
│     002       Red dye 109            25 gals              │
│     003       Wheel 12"              120 each             │
│     004       Plastic #4             300 lbs              │
│     005       Yellow dye 110         5 gals               │
│     006       Yellow dye 65          30 gals              │
│     007       Strut 15"              99 each              │
│     008       Axle 18"               250 each             │
│     009       Blue dye 25            18 gals              │
│     010       Plastic #8             350 lbs              │
│     011       Cotter pin small       515 each             │
│     012       Cotter pin medium      109 each             │
└─────────────────────────────────────────────────────────┘
```

Figure 9-7:   Mighty-Mite Motors raw materials inventory screen layout

to continue, which to discontinue, which to redesign, and which to recall.

MMM does not repair its own products. When a problem report is received, the customer is either directed to return the product to the store where it was purchased for an exchange (during the first 30 days after purchase) or directed to an authorized repair center in the customer's area. In the latter case, the problem report is faxed to the repair center so that it is waiting when the customer arrives. MMM does not plan to change this procedure because it currently provides quick, excellent service to customers and alleviates the need for MMM to stock replacement parts. (Replacement parts are stocked by the authorized repair centers.)

Product test results are recorded on paper forms (Figure 9-10). After a testing period is completed, the forms are collated manually to produce a summary of how well a new product performed. MMM would like the test results stored within an information system so that the testing report can be produced automatically, saving time and effort. Such a report will be used to help decide which new models should be placed in production.

Please register your Mighty-Mite Motors vehicle

By registering you receive the following benefits:

- Validation of the warranty on your vehicle, making it easier to obtain warranty service if ever necessary.
- Notification of product updates relating to your vehicle.
- Information mailings about enhancements to your vehicle and other products that may be of interest.

First name

Last name

Street

City   State   Zip

Phone #:

Model #   Serial #

Age of primary user of vehicle: _____

Gender: ☐ Male   ☐ Female

Date of purchase: ☐☐ ☐☐ ☐☐

Place of purchase:

Where did you first learn about Mighty-Mite Motors?

☐ Advertisement in a magazine or newspaper
☐ Friend's recommendation
☐ In-store display
☐ Catalog
☐ Other

What features of the vehicle prompted your purchase?

☐ Size
☐ Color
☐ Speed
☐ Safety features
☐ Cost
☐ Other

What is the relationship of the purchaser to the primary user?

☐ Parent
☐ Grandparent
☐ Aunt/Uncle
☐ Friend
☐ Other

Fold Here. Tape closed; do not staple.

Figure 9-8:   Mighty-Mite Motors purchase registration form

Designing the Database

The most effecitve approach to the design of a database (or collection of databases) for an environment as diverse as that presented by Mighty-Mite Motors usually involves breaking the design into components indicated by the organization of the company. As the design evolves, the designer can examine the entities and their relationships to determine where parts of the organization will need to share data. Working on one portion of the design at a time also sim-

Problem Report

Date   Time

First name

Last name

Street

City   State   Zip

Phone #:

Model #   Serial #

Problem Description:

Figure 9-9:   Mighty-Mite Motors problem report

plifies dealing with what might at first seem to be an overwhelmingly large database environment.

The Mighty-Mite Motors database environment seems to fall naturally into the following areas:

- Manufacturing (including finished goods inventory and raw materials ordering)
- Sales to toy stores and shipping of products ordered
- Reported purchases

Product Test Report

Date   Time

Location

Model tested:

Test type:

Test description

Test result and comments:

Figure 9-10:   Mighty-Mite Motors product test report

♦ Testing
♦ Problem handling

Examining the Data Flows

In this particular situation, a data flow diagram can be of enormous use in identifying where data are shared by various parts of an organization. The top-level DFD (the *context diagram*) in Figure 9-11 actually tells us very little. It indicates that three sources outside the company provide data: customers (the stores to which the company sells), purchasers (the individuals who purchase products from the stores), and raw materials suppliers. Somehow, all that data is used by a general process named "Manufacture & Sell Products" to keep the company in business.

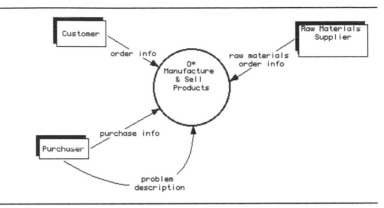

Figure 9-11:   Context DFD for Mighty-Mite Motors

However, the level 1 DFD (Figure 9-12) is much more telling. As the data handling processes are broken down, five data stores emerge:

- ◆ Raw materials: This data store holds both the raw materials inventory and the orders for raw materials.
- ◆ Product data: The product data store contains data about the products being manufactured and the finished goods inventory.
- ◆ Customer orders: This data store contains customer information as well as order data.
- ◆ Purchaser data: The purchaser data store contains information about the individuals who purchase products and the products they have purchased.
- ◆ Problem data: This final data store contains problem reports.

As you examine the processes that interact with these five data stores, you will find a number of processes that manipulate data in more than one data store as well as data stores that are used by more than one process:

- ◆ The raw materials data store is used by the raw materials ordering and the manufacturing processes.
- ◆ Product data are used by manufacturing, sales, shipping, and purchaser registration.

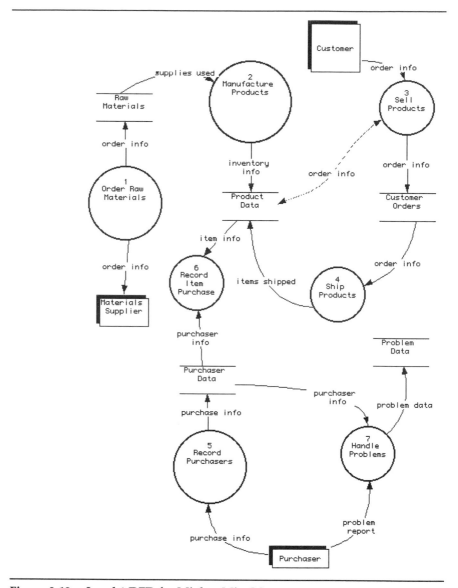

Figure 9-12:   **Level 1 DFD for Mighty-Mite Motors**

- Customer order data are used by sales and shipping.
- The purchaser data store is used by purchaser registration and problem handling.

♦ The problem data store, used only by problem handling, is the only data store not shared by multiple processes.

The raw materials ordering process is the only process that uses only a single data store. Nonetheless, the level 1 DFD makes it very clear that there is no instance in which a single process uses a single data store without interaction with other data stores and processes. Given that each process in the DFD probably represents all or part of an application program, this suggests that the database designer should probably consider a single database, rather than a set of databases.

The DFD makes it very clear that the need for the integration of the various data stores is very strong. In addition, Mighty-Mite Motors is a relatively small business and therefore a single database that manages all needed aspects of the company will not grow unreasonably large. Ultimately, the database designer may decide to distribute the database onto multiple servers, placing portions of it that are used most frequently in the divisions where that use occurs. The database design, however, will be the same regardless of whether the final implementation is centralized or distributed. The essential decision is to create a single database rather than several smaller, isolated databases that must somehow share data.

Creating the ER Diagram

The database designer working for Mighty-Mite Motors has two very good sources of information about exactly what needs to be stored in the database: the employees of the company and the paper documents the company has been using.

The designer needs to capture all the information on the paper documents. Some documents are used only for input (for example, the product registration form or the order form). Others represent outputs that an application program must be able to generate (for example, the line schedule report). Although the current documents do not necessarily represent all the outputs application programs running against the database will eventually prepare, they do provide a good starting place for the database design. Whenever the designer has questions, he or she can then turn to Mighty-Mite's employees for clarification.

Working from the documents, information gathered from employees, and the data flow diagram, the database developer puts together the ER diagram. Because there are so many entities, all of which interconnect, the diagram is very wide. It has therefore been split into three pieces so you can see it. As you look at each piece, keep in mind that entities that appear in more than one piece represent the connections between the three illustrations.

The first part (found in Figure 9-13) contains the entities for raw materials and manufacturing. This portion of the data model is dealing with three many-to-many relationships:

- material_order to raw_material (resolved by the composite entity material_order_line)
- raw_material to model (resolved by the composite entity material_needed)
- manufacturing_line to model (resolved by the composite entity line_schedule)

The second portion of the ERD (Figure 9-14) contains entities for product testing and sales. (Remember that in this instance, the customers are toy stores rather than individual purchasers.) There are two many-to-many relationships:

- test_type to model (resolved by the test entity)
- order to model (resolved by the order_line composite entity).

In this instance, the test entity is not a composite entity. It is an activity that someone performs and as such has an existence outside the database. It is not an entity created just to resolve a many-to-many relationship.

At this point the diagrams become a bit unusual, because of the need to keep track of individual products rather than simply

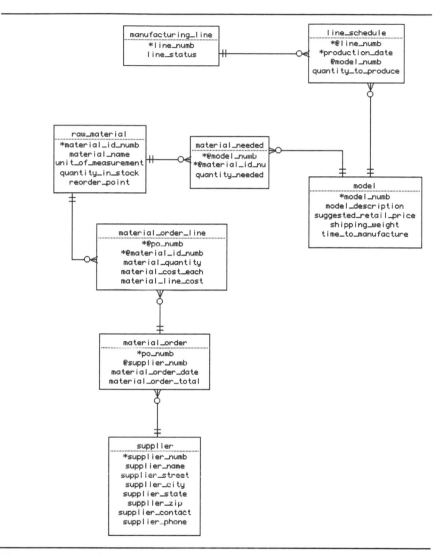

Figure 9-13: Mighty-Mite Motors ERD (part I)

groups of products of the same model. The model entity, which you first saw in Figure 9-13, represents a type of vehicle manufactured by Might-Mite Motors. However, the product entity, which first appears in Figure 9-14, represents a single vehicle that is uniquely identified by a serial number. This means that the relationships between an order, the line items on an order, and the models and

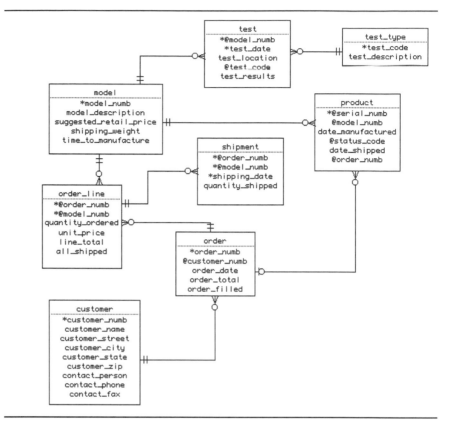

Figure 9-14:   Mighty-Mite Motors ERD (part II)

products are more complex than for most other sales database designs.

The order and line_item entities are fairly typical. They indicate how many of a given model are required to full a given order. The shipment entity then indicates how many of a specific model are shipped on a specific date. However, the database must also track the order in which individual products are shipped. As a result, there is a direct relationship between the product entity and the order entity, in addition to the relationships between order_line and model. In this way Mighty-Mite Motors will know exactly where each product has gone. At the same time, the company will be able to track the status of orders (in particular, how many units of each model have yet to ship).

The final portion of the ERD (Figure 9-15) deals with the purchasers and problem reports. There are two many-to-many relationships:

♦ problem_type to product (resolved with the entity problem_report)
♦ purchase to feature (resolved with the composite entity purchase_feature)

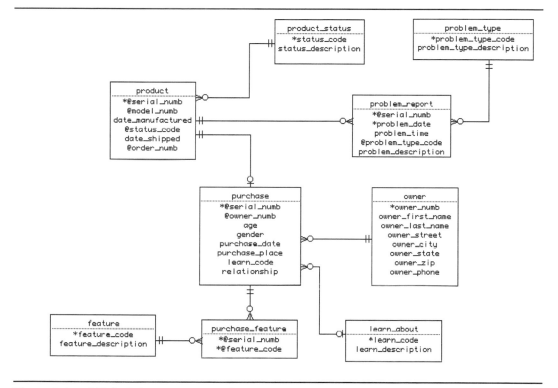

Figure 9-15:   Might-Mite Motors ERD (part III)

As with the test entity that you saw earlier, the problem_report entity acts like a composite entity to resolve a many-to-many relationship but is really a simple entity. It is an entity that has an existence outside the database and was not created simply to take care of the M:N relationship.

> *Note: Calling an entity "problem_report" can be a bit mislead-ing. In this case, the word "report" does not refer to a piece of paper but to the action of reporting a problem. A "problem_report" is therefore an activity rather than a docu-ment. In fact, the printed documentation of a problem report will probably include data from several entities, including the product, problem_report, purchase, and owner entities.*

If you look closely at the diagram, you'll notice that there is a one-to-one relationship between the product and purchase entities. The handling of the data supplied by a purchaser on the product regis-tration card presents an interesting dilemma for a database design-er. Each product will be registered by only one purchaser. (Even if the product is later sold or given to someone else, the new owner will not have a registration card to send in.) There will be only one set of registration data for each product, at first thought suggesting that all the registration data should be part of the product entity.

However, there is a *lot* of registration data—including one repeat-ing group (the features for which the purchaser chose the product, represented by the feature and purchase_feature entities)—and the product is involved in a number of relationships that have nothing to do with product registration. If the DBMS has to retrieve the reg-istration data along with the rest of the product data, database per-formance will suffer. It therefore makes sense in this case to keep the purchase data separate and to retrieve it only when absolutely needed.

> *Note: One common mistake made by novice database designers is to create an entity called a "registration card." It is important to remember that the card itself is merely an input document. What is crucial is the data the card contains and the entity those data describe, rather than the medium on which the data are supplied.*

Creating the Tables

The tables for the Mighty-Mite Motors database can come directly from the ER diagram. They are as follows:

```
model (model_numb, model_description, suggested_retail_price,
    shipping_weight, time_to_manufacture)
test (model_numb, test_date, test_location, test_code, test_results)
test_types (test_code, test_description)
customers (customer_numb, customer_name, customer_street,
    customer_street, customer_city, customer_state, customer_zip,
    contact_person, contact_phone, contact_fax)
orders (order_numb, customer_numb, order_date, order_total,
    order_filled)
order_line (order_numb, model_numb, quantity_ordered, unit_price,
    line_total, all_shipped)
shipments (order_numb, model_numb, shipping_date, quantity_shipped)
product (serial_numb, model_numb, date_manufactured, status_code,
    order_numb, date_shipped)
product_status (status_code, status_description)
raw_material (material_id_numb, material_name, unit_of_measurement,
    quantity_in_stock, reorder_point)
supplier (supplier_numb, supplier_name, supplier_street,
    supplier_city, supplier_state, supplier_zip, supplier_contact,
    supplier_phone)
material_order (po_numb, supplier_numb, material_order_date,
    material_order_total)
material_order_line (po_numb, material_id_numb, material_quantity,
    material_cost_each, material_line_cost)
material_needed (model_numb, material_id_numb, quantity_needed)
manufacturing_line (line_numb, line_status)
line_schedule (line_numb, production_date, model_numb,
    quantity_to_produce)
owner (owner_numb, owner_first_name, owner_last_name, owner_street,
    owner_city, owner_state, owner_zip, owner_phone)
purchase (serial_numb, owner_numb, age, gender, purchase_date,
    purchase_place, learn_code, relationship)
purchase_feature (serial_numb, feature_code)
learn_about (learn_code, learn_description)
feature (feature_code, feature_description)
problem_report (serial_numb, problem_date, problem_time,
    problem_type_code, problem_description)
problem_type (problem_type_code, problem_type_description)
```

Generating the SQL

Assuming that the designers of the Mighty-Mite Motors database are working with a CASE tool, then generating SQL statements to create the database can be automated. For example, in Figure 9-16 you will find the SQL generated by Mac A&D from the ER diagram you saw earlier in this chapter.

```
CREATE TABLE model
(
    model_numb INTEGER,
    model_description CHAR (40),
    suggested_retail_price DECIMAL (6,2),
    shipping_weight DECIMAL (6,2),
    time_to_manufacture TIME,
    PRIMARY KEY (model_numb)
);

CREATE TABLE test_type
(
    test_code INTEGER,
    test_description CHAR (40),
    PRIMARY KEY (test_code)
);

CREATE TABLE test
(
    model_numb INTEGER,
    test_date DATE,
    test_location CHAR (40),
    test_code INTEGER,
    test_results CHAR (40),
    PRIMARY KEY (model_numb, test_date),
    FOREIGN KEY (model_numb) REFERENCES model,
    FOREIGN KEY (test_code) REFERENCES test_type
);
```

Figure 9-16:   SQL statements needed to create the Mighty-Mite Motors database

```
CREATE TABLE customer
(
    customer_numb INTEGER,
    customer_name CHAR (40),
    customer_street CHAR (40),
    customer_city CHAR (30),
    customer_state CHAR (2),
    customer_zip CHAR (5),
    contact_person CHAR (40)CHAR (30),
    contact_phone CHAR (12),
    contact_fax CHAR (12),
    PRIMARY KEY (customer_numb)
);

CREATE TABLE order
(
    order_numb INTEGER,
    customer_numb INTEGER,
    order_date DATE,
    order_total DECIMAL (8,2),
    order_filled CHAR (1),
    PRIMARY KEY (order_numb),
    FOREIGN KEY (customer_numb) REFERENCES customer
);

CREATE TABLE order_line
(
    order_numb INTEGER,
    model_numb INTEGER,
    quantity_ordered INTEGER,
    unit_price DECIMAL (6,2),
    line_total DECIMAL (8,2),
    all_shipped CHAR (1),
    PRIMARY KEY (order_numb, model_numb),
    FOREIGN KEY (order_numb) REFERENCES order,
    FOREIGN KEY (model_numb) REFERENCES model
);
```

Figure 9-16: (Continued)   SQL statements needed to create the Mighty-Mite Motors database

```
CREATE TABLE shipment
(
    order_numb INTEGER,
    model_numb INTEGER,
    shipping_date DATE,
    quantity_shipped INTEGER,
    PRIMARY KEY (order_numb, model_numb, shipping_date),
    FOREIGN KEY (order_numb) REFERENCES order_line,
    FOREIGN KEY (model_numb) REFERENCES order_line
);

CREATE TABLE product
(
    serial_numb INTEGER,
    model_numb INTEGER,
    date_manufactured DATE,
    status_code INTEGER,
    date_shipped DATE,
    order_numb INTEGER,
    PRIMARY KEY (serial_numb),
    FOREIGN KEY (serial_numb) REFERENCES purchase,
    FOREIGN KEY (model_numb) REFERENCES model,
    FOREIGN KEY (status_code) REFERENCES product_status,
    FOREIGN KEY (order_numb) REFERENCES order
);

CREATE TABLE product_status
(
    status_code INTEGER,
    status_description CHAR (40),
    PRIMARY KEY (status_code)
);

CREATE TABLE raw_material
(
    material_id_numb INTEGER,
    material_name CHAR (30),
    unit_of_measurement CHAR (12),
    quantity_in_stock INTEGER,
    reorder_point INTEGER,
    PRIMARY KEY (material_id_numb)
);
```

Figure 9-16: (Continued)   SQL statements needed to create the Mighty-Mite Motors database

```
CREATE TABLE material_needed
(
    model_numb INTEGER,
    material_id_numb INTEGER,
    quantity_needed INTEGER,
    PRIMARY KEY (model_numb, material_id_numb),
    FOREIGN KEY (model_numb) REFERENCES model,
    FOREIGN KEY (material_id_numb) REFERENCES raw_material
);

CREATE TABLE supplier
(
    supplier_numb INTEGER,
    supplier_name CHAR (40),
    supplier_street CHAR (30),
    supplier_city CHAR (15),
    supplier_state CHAR (2),
    supplier_zip CHAR (5),
    supplier_contact CHAR (40),
    supplier_phone CHAR (12),
    PRIMARY KEY (supplier_numb)
);

CREATE TABLE material_order
(
    po_numb INTEGER,
    supplier_numb INTEGER,
    material_order_date DATE,
    material_order_total DECIMAL (6,2),
    PRIMARY KEY (po_numb),
    FOREIGN KEY (supplier_numb) REFERENCES supplier
);

CREATE TABLE material_order_line
(
    po_numb INTEGER,
    material_id_numb INTEGFR,
    material_quantity INTEGER,
    material_cost_each DECIMAL (6,2),
    material_line_cost DECIMAL (8,2),
    PRIMARY KEY (po_numb, material_id_numb),
    FOREIGN KEY (po_numb) REFERENCES material_order,
    FOREIGN KEY (material_id_numb) REFERENCES raw_material
);
```

Figure 9-16: (Continued)   SQL statements needed to create the Mighty-Mite Motors database

```
CREATE TABLE manufacturing_line
(
    line_numb INTEGER,
    line_status CHAR (12),
    PRIMARY KEY (line_numb)
);

CREATE TABLE line_schedule
(
    line_numb INTEGER,
    production_date DECIMAL (6,2)DATE,
    model_numb INTEGER,
    quantity_to_produce INTEGER,
    PRIMARY KEY (line_numb, production_date),
    FOREIGN KEY (line_numb) REFERENCES manufacturing_line,
    FOREIGN KEY (model_numb) REFERENCES model
);

CREATE TABLE owner
(
    owner_numb INTEGER,
    owner_first_name CHAR (15),
    owner_last_name CHAR (15),
    owner_street CHAR (30),
    owner_city CHAR (15),
    owner_state CHAR (2),
    owner_zip CHAR (5),
    owner_phone CHAR (12),
    PRIMARY KEY (owner_numb)
);

CREATE TABLE purchase
(
    serial_numb INTEGER,
    owner_numb INTEGER,
    age INTEGER,
    gender CHAR (1),
    purchase_date DATE,
    purchase_place CHAR (40),
    learn_code INTEGER,
    relationship CHAR (15),
    PRIMARY KEY (serial_numb),
    FOREIGN KEY (serial_numb) REFERENCES product,
    FOREIGN KEY (owner_numb) REFERENCES owner
);
```

Figure 9-16: (Continued)   SQL statements needed to create the Mighty-Mite Motors database

```
CREATE TABLE feature
(
    feature_code INTEGER,
    feature_description CHAR (40),
    PRIMARY KEY (feature_code)
);

CREATE TABLE purchase_feature
(
    serial_numb INTEGER,
    feature_code INTEGER,
    PRIMARY KEY (serial_numb, feature_code),
    FOREIGN KEY (serial_numb) REFERENCES purchase,
    FOREIGN KEY (feature_code) REFERENCES feature
);

CREATE TABLE learn_about
(
    learn_code INTEGER,
    learn_description CHAR (40),
    serial_numb INTEGER,
    PRIMARY KEY (learn_code),
    FOREIGN KEY (serial_numb) REFERENCES purchase
);

CREATE TABLE problem_type
(
    problem_type_code INTEGER,
    problem_type_description CHAR (30),
    PRIMARY KEY (problem_type_code)
);

CREATE TABLE problem_report
(
    serial_numb INTEGER,
    problem_date DATE,
    problem_time TIME,
    problem_type_code INTEGER,
    problem_description CHAR (40),
    PRIMARY KEY (serial_numb, problem_date),
    FOREIGN KEY (serial_numb) REFERENCES product,
    FOREIGN KEY (problem_type_code) REFERENCES problem_type
);
```

Figure 9-16: (Continued)   SQL statements needed to create the Mighty-Mite Motors database

10

Database Design Case Study #2: East Coast Aquarium

Many-to-many relationships are often the bane of the relational database designer. Sometimes it is not completely clear that you are dealing with that type of relationship. However, failure to recognize the many-to-many can result in serious data integrity problems.

The organization described in this chapter actually needs two databases, the larger of which is replete with many-to-many relationships. In some cases it will be necessary to create additional entities for composite entities to reference merely to ensure data integrity.

Perhaps the biggest challenge facing a database designer working for East Coast Aquarium is the lack of complete specifications. As you will read, the people who will be using the application programs created to manipulate the aquarium's two new databases have only a general idea of what they need the programs to do. Unlike Mighty-Mite Motors, which had the luxury of working from a large collection of existing forms and documents, East Coast Aquarium has nothing of that sort.

The situation therefore lends itself to a technique known as *prototyping*, in which the designers prepare the user interface of an application program and let the end users evaluate it. Based on user feedback, the designers modify the prototype until the output design matches what the users want. This iterative process helps the end users focus their requirements. The designers also gather the necessary information to create a database design that can provide the outputs the users need. A CASE tool that can model screen forms will therefore be an invaluable tool in preparing the prototype.

Organizational Overview

The East Coast Aquarium is a nonprofit organization dedicated to the study and preservation of marine life. Located on the Atlantic coast in the heart of a major northeastern U.S. city, it provides a wide variety of educational services to the surrounding area. The aquarium is supported by donations, memberships, charges for private functions, gift shop revenues, class fees, and the small admission fees it charges to the public. To help keep costs down, many of the public service jobs (leading tours, staffing the admissions counter, running the gift shop) are handled by volunteers.

The aquarium grounds consist of three buildings: the main facility, a dolphin house, and a marina where the aquarium's research barge is docked.

The centerpiece of the main building is a three-story center tank that is surrounded by a spiral walkway. The sides of the tank are primarily glass, so that visitors can walk around the tank, observing the residents at various depths.

Note: If you happen to recognize the layout of this aquarium, please keep in mind that only the physical structure of the environment is modeled after something that really exists. The way in which the organization functions is purely a product of the author's imagination and no commentary, positive or negative, is intended with regard to the real-world aquarium.

The height of the tank makes it possible to simulate the way in which habitats change as the ocean depth changes. Species that dwell on the ocean floor, coral reef fish, and sand bar dwellers therefore are all housed in the same tank, interacting in much the same way as they would in the ocean.

The remaining space on the first floor of the main building (Figure 10-1) includes the gift shop and a quarantine area for newly arrived animals. The latter area is not accessible to visitors.

The second floor (Figure 10-2) contains a classroom and the volunteers office. Small tanks containing single-habitat exhibits are installed in the outside walls. These provide places to house species that have special habitat requirements or that don't coexist well with other species.

The third floor (Figure 10-3) provides wall space for additional small exhibits. It also houses the aquarium's administrative offices.

East Coast Aquarium has two very different areas in which it needs data management. The first is in the handling of its animals— where they are housed in the aquarium, where they came from, what they are to be fed, problems that occur in the tanks, and so on. The second area concerns the volunteers, including who they are, what they have been trained to do, and when they are scheduled to work. For this particular organization, the two data enviroments are completely separate; they share no data. A database designer who volunteers to work with the aquarium staff will therefore prepare two database designs, one to be used by the volunteer staff in the volunteers office and another to be used by the administrative and animal-care staff through the aquarium grounds.

Figure 10-1   The first floor of East Coast Aquarium's main building

Animal Tracking Needs

Currently, East Coast Aquarium uses a general-purpose PC accounting package to handle its data processing needs. The software takes care of payroll as well as purchasing and the accompanying accounts payable. Because the aquarium is a nonprofit organization, it does not have accounts receivables as does a for-profit business.

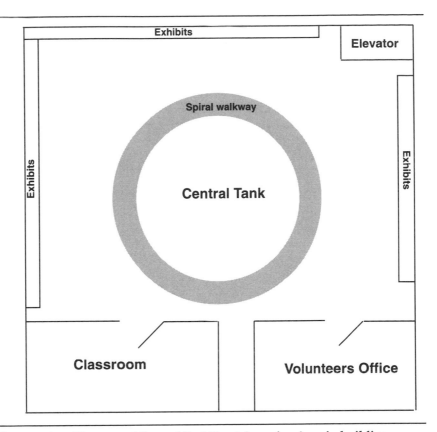

Figure 10-2::   The second floor of East Coast Aquarium's main building

Instead, income from the gift shop, admissions, and donations is handled on a cash basis. Grant income is managed by special-purpose software designed to monitor grant awards and how they are spent.

Although the accounting and grant management packages adquately handle the aquarium's finances, there is no data processing that tracks the actual animals housed in the aquarium. The three people in charge of the animals have expressed a need for the following:

♦ An "inventory" of which species are living in which locations in the aquarium. Some species can be found in more

Figure 10-3: The third floor of East Coast Aquarium's main building

than one tank, and several tanks in addition to the central tank contain more than one species. For larger animals, such as sharks and dolphins, the head animal keeper would like a precise count. However, for small fish that are often eaten by larger fish and that breed in large numbers, only an estimate is possible. The animal handling staff would like to be able to search for information about animals using either the animal's English name or its Latin name.

♦ Data about the foods each species eats, including how much should be fed at what interval. The head animal keeper would like to be able to print out a feeding instruction list every morning to give to staff. In addition, the animal-feeding staff would like to store information about their food inventory. Although the purchasing of food is handled by the administrative office, the head animal keeper would like an application program to decrement the food inventory automatically by the amount fed each day and to generate a tickle report whenever the stock level of a type of food drops below the reorder point. This will make it much easier to ensure that the aquarium does not run short of animal feed.

- Data about the sizes, locations, and habitats of the tanks on the aquarium grounds. Some tanks, such as the main tank, contain more than one habitat, and the same habitat can be found in more than one tank.

- Data about tank maintenance. Although the main tank is fed directly from the ocean, the smaller tanks around the walls of the main building are closed environments, much like a saltwater aquarium someone might have at home. This means that the pH and salinity of the tanks must be monitored closely. The head animal keeper therefore would like to print out a maintenance schedule each day as well as be able to keep track of what maintenance is actually performed.

- Data about the habitats in which a given species can live. When a new species arrives at the aquarium, the staff can use this information to determine which locations could possibly house that species.

- Data about where species can be obtained. If the aquarium wants to increase the population of a particular species and the increase cannot be generated through in-house breeding, then the staff would like to know which external supplier can be contacted. Some of the suppliers sell animals; others, such as zoos or other aquariums, will trade or donate animals.

- Problems that arise in the tanks. When animals become ill, the veterinarian wants to be able to view a history of both the animal and the tank in which it is currently living.

- Data about orders placed for animals and, in particular, the shipments in which animals arrive. Since any financial arrangements involved in securing animals are handled by the administrative office, these data indicate only how many individuals of each species are included on a given order or shipment.

The shipment and problem data are particularly important to the aquarium. When animals first arrive, they are not placed immediately into the general population. Instead, they are held in special tanks in the quarantine area at the rear of the aquarium's first floor. The length of the quarantine is determined by the species.

After the quarantine period has passed and the animals are declared disease free, they can be placed on exhibit in the main portion of the aquarium. Nonetheless, animals do become ill after they have been released from quarantine. It is therefore essential that records are kept of the sources of animals so that patterns of illness can be tracked back to specific suppliers, if such patterns appear. By the same token, patterns of illnesses in various species housed in the same tank can be an indication of serious problems with the environment in the tank.

The Volunteer Organization

The volunteer organization (the Friends of the Aquarium) is totally separate from the financial and animal-handling areas of the aquarium. Volunteers perform tasks that do not involve direct contact with animals, such as leading tours, manning the admissions desk, and running the gift shop. The aquarium has provided office space and a telephone line for the volunteer coordinator and her staff. Beyond that, the Friends of the Aquarium organization has been on its own to secure office furniture and equipment.

The recent donation of a PC now makes it possible for the volunteers to automate some of their scheduling. Currently, the scheduling processing works in the following way:

◆ The person on duty in the volunteers office receives requests for volunteer services from the aquarium's administrative office. Some of the jobs are regularly scheduled (for example, staffing the gift shop and the admissions desk). Others are ad hoc, such as the request by a school-teacher to bring a class of children for a tour.

- The volunteer doing the scheduling checks the list of volunteers to see who is trained to do the job requested. Each volunteer's information is recorded on an index card, along with the volunteer's skills. A skill is a general expression of something the volunteer knows how to do, such as lead a tour for elementary school children. The volunteer's information also includes an indication of when that person is available to work.

- The volunteer doing the scheduling separates the cards for those people who have the required skill and have indicated that they are available at the required time. Most volunteers work on a regularly scheduled basis either at the admissions desk or in the gift shop. However, for ad hoc jobs, the person doing the scheduling must start making telephone calls until someone who is willing and able to do the job is found.

- The volunteer is scheduled for the job by writing in the master schedule notebook. As far as the volunteer coordinator is concerned, a job is an application of a skill. Therefore, a skill is knowing how to lead a tour for elementary school students, while a job that applies that skill is leading a tour of Mrs. Brown's third graders at 10 AM on Thursday.

One of the things that is very difficult to do with the current scheduling process is to keep track of the work record of each individual volunteer. The aquarium holds a volunteer recognition luncheon once a year, and the volunteer organization would like to find an easy way to identify volunteers who have put in an extra effort so that they can be recognized at that event. In contrast, the volunteer organization would also like to be able to identify volunteers who rarely participate —the people who stay on the volunteer rolls only to get free admission to the aquarium—as well as people who make commitments to work but do not show up. (The latter are actually far more of a problem than the former.)

The Volunteers Database

In terms of scope, the volunteers database is considerably smaller than the animal tracking database. It therefore makes sense to tackle the smaller project first. The database designers will create the application prototype and review it with the users. When the users are satisfied and the designers feel they have enough detailed information to actually design a database, they will move on to the more traditional steps of creating an ER diagram, tables, and SQL statements.

> *Note: As you will see, there is a lot involved in creating a prototype. It requires very detailed intensive work and produces a significant number of diagrams. We will therefore look at the volunteers prototype in full, but in the interest of length we will look at only selected aspects of the animal tracking prototype.*

Creating the Application Prototype

Given that the specifications of the database are rather general, the first step is to create a prototype of an application program interface. It begins with the opening screen and its main menu bar (Figure 10-4). As you can see, when in browse mode, the CASE tool allows users and designers to pull down the menus in the menu bar.

The complete menu tree (with the exception of the Help menu, whose contents are determined by the user interface guidelines of the operating system on which the application is running) can be found in Figure 10-5. Looking at the menu options, users can see that their basic requirements have been fulfilled. The details, however, must be specified by providing users with specific output designs.

Each menu option in the prototype's main menu has therefore been linked to a screen form. For example, to modify or delete a volunteer, a user must first *find* the volunteer's data. Therefore the Modify or Delete a Volunteer menu option leads to a dialog box that allows

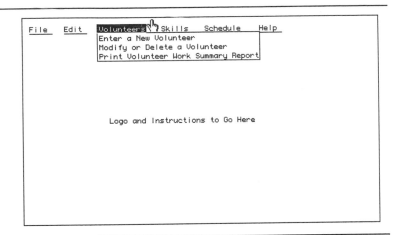

Figure 10-4:   Main menu prototype for the volunteers application

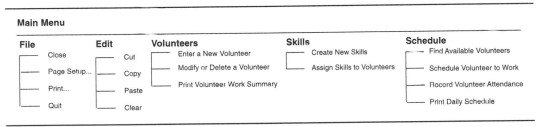

Figure 10-5:   Menu tree of the volunteers database prototype application

the user either to enter a volunteer number or to select a volunteer by name and phone number from a list (Figure 10-6). With the prototype, clicking the Find button opens the modify–delete form (Figure 10-7). Users can click in the data entry fields and tab between them, but the buttons at the right of the window are not functional.

While in browse mode, the CASE tool presents a form as it would appear to the user. However, in design mode, a database designer can see the names of the fields on the form (for example, Figure 10-8). These field names will ultimately guide the design of the database.

In the case of the volunteer data, it is apparent to the designers that there are at least two entities (and perhaps three) involved with the data that describe a volunteer. The first entity is represented by the

Figure 10-6: Prototype of a dialog box for finding a volunteer for modification

Figure 10-7: Prototype of a form for modifying and deleting a volunteer

single-valued fields occupying the top half of the form (volunteer number, first name, last name, street, city, state, zip, and phone). However, the availability data—day of the week, starting time, and ending time—are multivalued and therefore must be given an entity of their own. This also implies that there will be a one-to-many

Figure 10-8: Prototype data modification form showing field names

relationship between a volunteer and a period of time during which he or she is available.

> Note: Should you choose, the field names on a screen prototype can become part of the data dictionary. However, if the field names do not ultimately correspond to column names, their inclusion may add unnecessary complexity to the data dictionary.

The remainder of the prototype application and its forms are designed and analyzed in a similar way:

♦ The volunteer work summary report has been designed to let the user enter a range of dates that the report will cover (see Figure 10-9). The report itself (Figure 10-10) is a control-break report that displays the work performed by each volunteer along with the total hours worked and the number of times the volunteer was a "no show." The latter number was included because the volunteer coordinator had indicated that it was extremely important to know which volunteers consistently signed up to work and then didn't report when scheduled.

Figure 10-9: A dialog box layout for entering dates for the work summary report

Figure 10-10: Prototype layout for the work summary report

The need to report the "no shows" tells the designers that the schedule table needs to include a boolean column that indicates whether a person showed up for a scheduled shift. The report layout also includes some computed fields (total hours worked and number of no shows) that contain data that do not need to be stored but can be generated when the report is displayed.

♦ Entering a new skill into the master list of skills requires only a simple form (Figure 10-11). The end user sees only the description of a skill. However, the database designers know that the best way to handle unstructured blocks of text is to assign each description a skill number, which can then be used as a foreign key throughout the database. Users, however, do not necessarily need to know that a skill number is being used; they will always see just the text descriptions.

Figure 10-11   Entering a new skill

♦ To assign skills to a volunteer, the end user must first find the volunteer. The application can therefore use a copy of the dialog box in Figure 10-6. In this case, however, the Find button leads to the form in Figure 10-12.

Figure 10-12:   Assigning skills to a volunteer

A database designer will quickly recognize that there is a many-to-many relationship between a skill and a volunteer. There are actually three entities behind Figure 10-12: the skill, the volunteer, and the conposite entity that represents the relationship between the two. The skill entry form displays data from the volunteer entity at the top, data from the composite entity in the current skills list, and all skills not assigned from the skills table in the skill description list. Of course, the actual foreign key used in the composite entity is a skill number, but the user sees only the result of a join back to the skills table that retrieves the skill description.

> *Note: Database integrity constraints will certainly prevent anyone from assigning the same skill twice to the same volunteer. However, it is easier if the user can see currently assigned skills. Then, the application can restrict what appears in the skill description list to all skills not assigned to that volunteer. In this case, it is a matter of user interface design rather than database design.*

    ♦ To find the volunteers available to perform a specific job, the volunteers application needs a form something like Figure 10-13. The end user enters the date and time of the job and chooses the skill required by the job. Clicking the Search button fills in the table at the bottom of the form with the names and phone numbers of volunteers who are theoretically available.

Of all the outputs produced by this application, finding available volunteers is probably the most difficult to implement. The application program must not only work with overlapping intervals of time but also consider both when a volunteer indicates he or she will be available and when a volunteer is already scheduled to work. In most cases, however, a database designer does not have to write the application program code. The designer needs only to ensure that the data necessary to produce the output are present in the database.

> *Note: A smart database designer, however, would discuss any output that involves evaluating overlapping time intervals with application programmers to ensure that the output is feasible. There is no point in specifying infeasible output.*

    ♦ Once the person doing the volunteer scheduling has located a volunteer to fill a specific job, then the volunteer's

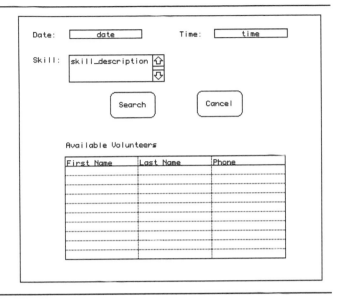

Figure 10-13: **Finding available volunteers**

commitment to work needs to become a part of the database. The process begins by presenting the user with a Find Volunteer dialog box like that in Figure 10-6. In this case, the Find button is linked to the Schedule Volunteer window (Figure 10-14). A database designer will recognize that this is not all the data that needs to be stored about a job, however. In particular, someone will need to record whether the volunteer actually appeared to do the scheduled job on the day of the job; this cannot be done when the job is scheduled initially.

♦ To record attendance, an end user first locates the volunteer using a Find Volunteer dialog box (Figure 10-6), which then leads to a display of the jobs the volunteer has been scheduled to work in reverse chronological order (see Figure 10-15). For those jobs that have not been worked, the End Time and Worked? columns will be empty. The user can then scroll the list to find the job to be modified and enter values for the two empty columns. The fields on this form, plus those on the job scheduling

Figure 10-14:   Scheduling a volunteer to perform a job

form, represent the attributes that will describe the job entity.

Figure 10-15:   Recording jobs worked

♦ To print a daily schedule, an end user first uses a dialog box to indicate the date for which a schedule should be displayed (Figure 10-16). The application program then assembles the report (Figure 10-17). To simplify working with the program, the application developers should probably allow users to double-click on any line in the listing to open the form in Figure 10-15 for the scheduled volunteer. However, this capability has no impact on the database design.

Figure 10-16:   Choosing a date for schedule display

Figure 10-17:   Volunteer work schedule

Creating the ER Diagram

From the approved prototype of the application design, the database designers can gather enough information to create a basic ER diagram for the volunteers organization. The designers examine each screen form carefully to ensure that the database design provides the attributes and relationships necessary to generate the output.

Although the application prototype consumes many screen forms, the underlying database design is surprisingly simple. The complete ER diagram can be found in Figure 10-18. The Skills Known entity serves as a composite entity between Volunteer and Skill. Given that there is no direct relationship between a skill and a job, then scheduling data (the Job entity) is related to the volunteer entity in a simple one-to-many relationship. The same is true of the availability data.

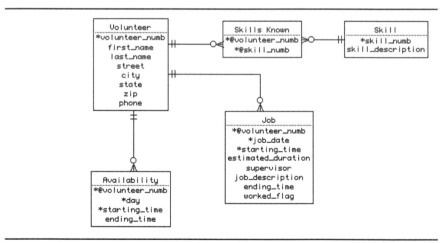

Figure 10-18:   ER diagram for the volunteers database

Designing the Tables

The ER diagram in Figure 10-18 produces the following tables:

```
Volunteer (volunteer_numb, first_name, last_name, street, city,
    state, zip, phone)
Availability (volunteer_numb, day, starting_time, ending_time)
```

```
Job (volunteer_numb, job_date, starting_time, estimated_duration,
    supervisor, job_description, ending_time, worked_flag)
Skill (skill_numb, skill_description)
Skills_known (volunteer_numb, skill_numb)
```

The Job table presents a question that must be answered before a correct primary key can be chosen. In particular, can a volunteer perform more than one job on a single day? If so, then the starting time must be concatenated with the volunteer number and the job date to form a unique primary key. However, if volunteers are limited to only one job in a given day, then the starting time does not need to be part of the key.

Generating the SQL

The five tables that make up the volunteers database can be created with the SQL in Figure 10-19. Notice that some of the attributes in the Volunteer table have been specified as NOT NULL. This constraint ensures that at least a name and phone number are available for each volunteer.

> Note: The domain of INTERVAL was introduced with the SQL-92 standard and may not be available with all of today's DMBSs. When INTERVALS are not available, you can store the duration of an event as an integer (number of minutes) that can later be added to a starting time.

The Animal Tracking Database

The animal tracking database is considerably larger than the volunteers database. The application that will manipulate that database therefore is concomitantly larger, as demonstrated by the menu tree in Figure 10-20. (The File and Edit menus have been left off so that the diagram will fit across the width of the page. However, they are intended to be the first and second menus from the left, respectively. A Help menu can also be added along the right edge.)

```
CREATE TABLE volunteer
(
    volunteer_numb INT,
    first_name CHAR (15) NOT NULL,
    last_name CHAR (15) NOT NULL,
    street CHAR (30),
    city CHAR (15),
    state CHAR (2),
    zip CHAR (5),
    phone CHAR (12) NOT NULL,
    PRIMARY KEY (volunteer_numb) );

CREATE TABLE availability
(
    volunteer_numb INT,
    day CHAR (10),
    starting_time TIME,
    ending_time TIME,
    PRIMARY KEY (volunteer_numb, day, starting_time),
    FOREIGN KEY (volunteer_numb) REFERENCES volunteer );

CREATE TABLE skill
(
    skill_numb INT,
    skill_description CHAR (30),
    PRIMARY KEY (skill_numb) );

CREATE TABLE skills_known
(
    volunteer_numb INT,
    skill_numb INT,
    PRIMARY KEY (volunteer_numb, skill_numb),
    FOREIGN KEY (volunteer_numb) REFERENCES volunteer,
    FOREIGN KEY (skill_numb) REFERENCES skill );

CREATE TABLE Job
(
    volunteer_numb INT,
    job_date DATE,
    starting_time TIME,
    estimated_duration INTERVAL,
    supervisor CHAR (30),
    job_description CHAR (255),
    ending_time TIME,
    worked_flag CHAR (1),
    PRIMARY KEY (volunteer_numb, job_date, starting_time),
    FOREIGN KEY (volunteer_numb) REFERENCES volunteer );
```

Figure 10-19: **SQL statements needed to create the tables for the volunteers database**

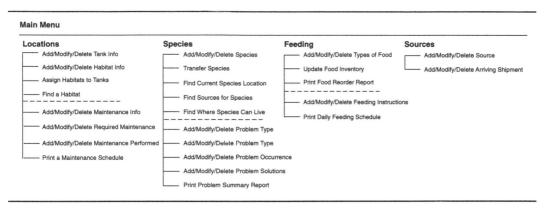

Figure 10-20:   Menu tree for the animal tracking database

The functionality requested by the animal handlers falls generally into four categories: the locations (the tanks) and their habitats, the species, the food, and the sources for animals. The organization of the application interface was therefore guided by those groupings.

Highlights of the Application Prototype

The screen and report layouts designed for the animal tracking application provide a good starting place for the database designers to identify the entities and attributes needed in the database. As with the volunteers application, there is not necessarily a one-to-one correspondence between an entity and an output.

> Note: One of the common mistakes novices make when designing the interfaces of database application programs is to use one data entry form per table. Users do not look at their environment in the same way as a database designer, however, and often the organization imposed by tables does not make sense to the users. Another benefit of prototype is therefore that it forces database and application designers to adapt to what the users really need, rather than the other way around.

Food Management

One of the important functions mentioned by the aquarium's animal handlers was management of the animal feeding schedule and the food inventory. First, they wanted a daily feeding schedule, such as that in Figure 10-21. Knowing that each species can eat many types of food and that a type of food can be eaten by many species, a database designer realizes that there are at least four entities behind the sample output:

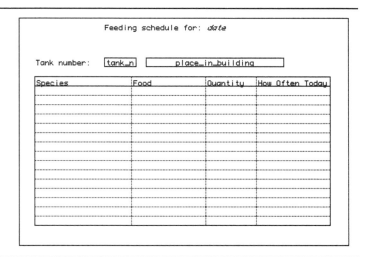

Figure 10-21: Daily feeding schedule

♦ An entity that indicates which species lives in which tank (a composite entity between the tank and species entities).
♦ An entity describing a type of food.
♦ An entity describing a species.
♦ An entity that indicates which species eats which food and how often that food should be fed (a composite entity between the food and species entities).

Food inventory management—although it sounds like a separate function to the animal handlers—actually requires nothing more than the food entity. The food entity needs to store data about how much food is currently in stock and a reorder point. The application program can take care of decrementing how much has been fed when the animal handlers run the Update Food Inventory function.

Handling Arriving Animals

When a shipment arrives at the aquarium, animal handlers first check the contents of the shipment against the shipment's paperwork. They then take the animals and place them in the aquarium's quarantine area. The data entry form that the animal handlers will use to store data about arrivals therefore includes a place for entering an identifier for the tank in which the new animals have been placed (Figure 10-22). Given that the aquarium staff needs to be able to locate animals at any time, this suggests that the quarantine tanks should be handled no differently from the exhibit tanks and that there is only one entity for a tank.

Figure 10-22: Recording the arrival of a shipment of animals

After the quarantine period has expired and the animals are certified as healthy, they can be transferred to another location in the building. This means an application program must delete the species from their current tank (regardless of whether it is a quarantine tank or an exhibit tank) and insert data for the new tank. The screen form (Figure 10-23) therefore lets the user identify the species and its current location using popup menus. The user also uses a popup menu to indicate the new location. To a database designer, this translates into the deletion of one row from a table—a table representing a composite entity between tank and species entities—and an insertion of a new row. All the database design needs to do, however, is provide the table; the application program will take care of managing the data modification.

Figure 10-23:   Moving a species between tanks

Problem Analysis

The health of the animals in the aquarium is a primary concern of the animal handlers. They are therefore anxious to be able to analyze the problems that occur in the tanks for patterns. Perhaps a single species is experiencing more problems than any other; perhaps an animal handler is not paying as much attention to the condition of the tanks for which he or she is responsible.

The animal handlers want the information in Figure 10-24 included in the problem summary report. What cannot be seen from the sample screen created by the CASE tool is that the data will appear in a control-break layout. For example, each tank number will appear only once; each species will appear once for each tank in which it was the victim of a problem. By the same token, each type of problem will appear once for each tank and species it affected. Only the problem solutions will contain data for every row in the sample output table.

Figure 10-24:   Problem summary report

To a database designer, the form in Figure 10-24 suggests the need for five entities:

♦ The species
♦ The tank
♦ The type of problem
♦ A problem occurrence (a type of problem occurring in one tank and involving one species)
♦ A problem solution (a solution that has been tried for one problem occurrence). There may be many solutions to a single problem occurrence.

One of the best ways to handle problems is to avoid them. For this reason, the animal handlers also want to include maintenance data in their database. To make data entry simpler for the end users, the form for entering required maintenance (Figure 10-25) allows a user to select a tank and then enter as many maintenance activities as needed.

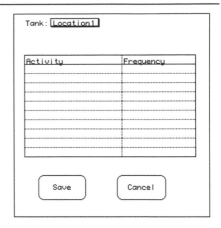

Figure 10-25:   Entering required maintenance

A database designer views such a form as requiring three entities: the tank, the maintenance activity, and the maintenance required for the tank (a composite entity between the tank and maintenance activity entities.)

Creating the ER Diagram

After refining the entire application prototype, the database designers for the East Coast Aquarium generate a large interconnected ER diagram. (Part I can be found in Figure 10-26; part II appears in Figure 10-27.) As you can see when examining both diagrams, the centerpiece is the Species entity, which participates in six different relationships.

There are at least 10 many-to-many relationships represented by this design:

- Species to Location
- Location to Habitat
- Species to Habitat
- Location to Maintenance Activity for required maintenance
- Location to Maintenance Activity for maintenance performed

Figure 10-26:   Animal handling ERD (part I)

- Location to Problem
- Species to Problem
- Species to Food
- Species to Source for ability of source to supply the species
- Shipment to Species

The relationships involving Location, Problem, and Species are particularly interesting. On the surface, there appears to be a many-to-many relationship between a tank and a type of problem. By the same token, there appears to be another many-to-many relationship between a species and a type of problem. The problem is that if the database maintains the two separate relationships, each with its own individual composite entity, then it will be impossible to determine which species was affected by which problem in which tank. To resolve the issue, the design uses a three-way composite entity—Problem Occurrence—that relates three parent entities (Location, Problem, and Species) rather than just the traditional two. Semantically, a problem occurrence is one type of problem affecting one

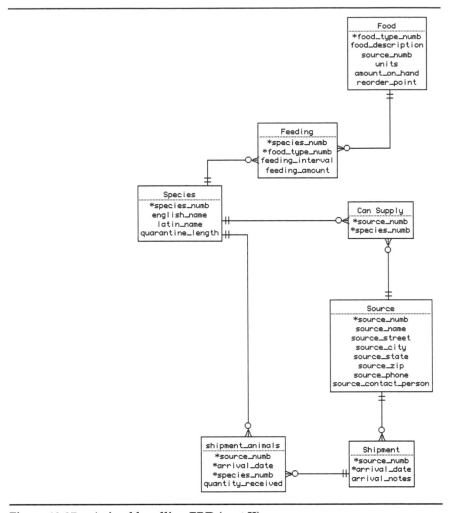

Figure 10-27:   Animal handling ERD (part II)

species in one location and therefore identifying it in the database requires all three parent entities.

In contrast, why is there no three-way composite entity between Species, Location, and Habitat? As with the preceding example, there is a many-to-many relationship between Species and Location and a many-to-many relationship between Habitat and Location. The answer once again lies in the meaning of the relationships.

Were we to create a single composite entity relating all three entities, we would be asserting that a given species lives in a given habitat in a given location. However, the animal handlers at the aquarium know that this type of data is not valid, particularly because if an animal lives in a tank with many habitats, the animal may move between multiple habitats. Instead, the relationship between Species and Habitat indicates all habitats in which a species can live successfully; the relationship between Location and Habitat indicates the habitats provided by a tank.

The remainder of the many-to-many relationships are the typical two-parent relationships that you have been seeing throughout this book. The only aspect of these relationships that is the least bit unusual is the two relationships between Maintenance Activity and Location. Each relationship has a different meaning (scheduled maintenance versus maintenance actually performed). Therefore, the design must include two composite entities, one to represent the meaning of each individual relationship.

> Note: There is no theoretical restriction to the number of relationships that can exist between the same parent entities. As long as each relationship has a different meaning, then there is usually justification for including all of them in a database design.

Creating the Tables

The ER diagrams translate to the following tables:

```
species (species_numb, english_name, latin_name, quarantine_length)
location (tank_numb, place_in_building, fluid_capacity)
population (species_numb, tank_numb, number_of_animals)
habitat (habitat_numb, habitat_description)
can_live_in (species_numb, habitat_numb)
habitats_contained (tank_numb, habitat_numb)
problem (problem_type_numb, problem_description)
problem_occurrence (problem_numb, problem_date, tank_numb,
    species_numb, problem_type_numb)
problem_solution (problem_numb, solution_date, solution_applied)
source (source_numb, source_name, source_street, source_city,
    source_state, source_zip, source_phone, source_contact_person)
can_supply (source_numb, species_numb)
shipment (source_numb, shipment_date, arrival_notes)
```

```
shipment_animals (source numb, arrival date, species numb,
    quantity_received)
food (food type numb, food_description, source_numb, units,
    amount_on_hand, reorder_point)
feeding (species numb, food type numb, feeding_interval,
    feeding_amount)
maintenance_activity (activity numb, activity_description)
maintenance_required (activity numb, tank numb, how_often)
maintenance_performed (activity numb, tank numb, activity_date)
```

Choosing a primary key for the problem occurrence table presents a bit of a dilemma. Given that a problem occurrence represents a relationship between a problem type, tank, and species, the theoretically appropriate primary key is a concatenation of the problem type number, tank number, species number, and the date of the problem. However, this is an extremely awkward primary key to use as a foreign key in the Problem Solution table. Although it is unusual to give composite entities arbitrary unique identifiers, in this case it makes good practical sense.

There are several tables in this design that are "all key" (made up of nothing but the primary key). According to the CASE tool used to draw the ER diagram, this represents an error in the design. However, there is nothing in relational database theory that states that all-key relations are not allowed. In fact, they are rather common when they are needed to represent a many-to-many relationship that has no accompanying relationship data.

Generating the SQL

The SQL CREATE statements that generate the animal tracking database for East Coast Aquarium can be found in Figure 10-28. Because of the large number of composite entities, there are also a large number of foreign keys. Other than that, the SQL presents no unusual features.

```
CREATE TABLE species
(
    species_numb INT,
    english_name CHAR (100),
    latin_name CHAR (100),
    quarantine_length INT,
    PRIMARY KEY (species_numb) );

CREATE TABLE location
(
    tank_numb INT,
    place_in_building CHAR (30),
    fluid_capacity DECIMAL (9,2),
    PRIMARY KEY (tank_numb) );

CREATE TABLE can_live_in
(
    species_numb INT,
    habitat_numb INT,
    PRIMARY KEY (species_numb, habitat_numb),
    FOREIGN KEY (species_numb) REFERENCES species,
    FOREIGN KEY (habitat_numb) REFERENCES habitat );

CREATE TABLE population
(
    species_numb INT,
    tank_numb INT,
    number_of_animals INT,
    PRIMARY KEY (species_numb, tank_numb),
    FOREIGN KEY (species_numb) REFERENCES species,
    FOREIGN KEY (tank_numb) REFERENCES location );

CREATE TABLE habitat
(
    habitat_numb INT,
    habitat_description CHAR (100),
    PRIMARY KEY (habitat_numb) );

CREATE TABLE problem
(
    problem_type_numb INT,
    problem_description CHAR (100),
    PRIMARY KEY (problem_type_numb) );
```

Figure 10-28:   SQL statements to create the animal handing database

```
CREATE TABLE problem_occurrence
(
    problem_numb INT,
    problem_date DATE,
    tank_numb INT,
    species_numb INT,
    problem_type_numb INT,
    PRIMARY KEY (problem_numb),
    FOREIGN KEY (tank_numb) REFERENCES location,
    FOREIGN KEY (species_numb) REFERENCES species,
    FOREIGN KEY (problem_type_numb) REFERENCES problem );

CREATE TABLE problem_solution
(
    problem_numb INT,
    solution_date DATE,
    solution_applied CHAR (100),
    PRIMARY KEY (problem_numb, solution_date),
    FOREIGN KEY (problem_numb) REFERENCES problem_occurrence );

CREATE TABLE source
(
    source_numb INT,
    source_name CHAR (30),
    source_street CHAR (30),
    source_city CHAR (30),
    source_state CHAR (2),
    source_zip CHAR (5),
    source_phone CHAR (12),
    source_contact_person CHAR (30),
    PRIMARY KEY (source_numb) );

CREATE TABLE shipment
(
    source_numb INT,
    arrival_date DATE,
    arrival_notes CHAR (255),
    PRIMARY KEY (source_numb, arrival_date),
    FOREIGN KEY (source_numb) REFERENCES source );

CREATE TABLE can_supply
(
    source_numb INT,
    species_numb INT,
    PRIMARY KEY (source_numb, species_numb),
    FOREIGN KEY (source_numb) REFERENCES source,
    FOREIGN KEY (species_numb) REFERENCES species );
```

Figure 10-28: (Continued) SQL statements to create the animal handing database

```
CREATE TABLE shipment_animals
(
    source_numb INT,
    arrival_date DATE,
    species_numb INT,
    quantity_received INT,
    PRIMARY KEY (source_numb, arrival_date, species_numb),
    FOREIGN KEY (source_numb) REFERENCES shipment,
    FOREIGN KEY (arrival_date) REFERENCES shipment,
    FOREIGN KEY (species_numb) REFERENCES species );

CREATE TABLE food
(
    food_type_numb INT,
    food_description CHAR (30),
    source_numb INT,
    units CHAR (15),
    amount_on_hand INT,
    reorder_point INT,
    PRIMARY KEY (food_type_numb) );

CREATE TABLE feeding
(
    species_numb INT,
    food_type_numb INT,
    feeding_interval CHAR (15),
    feeding_amount CHAR (15),
    PRIMARY KEY (species_numb, food_type_numb),
    FOREIGN KEY (species_numb) REFERENCES species,
    FOREIGN KEY (food_type_numb) REFERENCES food );

CREATE TABLE habitats_contained
(
    tank_numb INT,
    habitat_numb INT,
    PRIMARY KEY (tank_numb, habitat_numb),
    FOREIGN KEY (tank_numb) REFERENCES location,
    FOREIGN KEY (habitat_numb) REFERENCES habitat );

CREATE TABLE maintenance_activity
(
    activity_numb INT,
    activity_description CHAR (30),
    PRIMARY KEY (activity_numb) );
```

Figure 10-28: (Continued)   SQL statements to create the animal handing database

```
CREATE TABLE maintenance_required
(
    activity_numb INT,
    tank_numb INT,
    how_often INTERVAL,
    PRIMARY KEY (activity_numb, tank_numb),
    FOREIGN KEY (activity_numb) REFERENCES maintenance_activity,
    FOREIGN KEY (tank_numb) REFERENCES location
);

CREATE TABLE maintenance_performed
(
    activity_numb INT,
    tank_numb INT,
    activity_date DATE,
    PRIMARY KEY (activity_numb, tank_numb, activity_date),
    FOREIGN KEY (activity_numb) REFERENCES maintenance_activity,
    FOREIGN KEY (tank_numb) REFERENCES location
);
```

Figure 10-28: (Continued)   SQL statements to create the animal handing database

11

Database Design Case Study #3: Independent Intelligence Agency

In the preceding two case studies, we have encountered several database design challenges, including the need to determine whether one or more databases are required, incomplete specifications, and a large number of many-to-many relationships. The final case study we are going to consider presents two different challenges: First, the specifications have been written by people who are more concerned with security than they are with helping database designers; second, the environment contains an enormous number of repeating groups. In addition, this is the largest database you have seen so far. Although at the outset it may appear that there are two or three separate databases, the parts of the database share just enough data that the only way to meet all the organization's requirements is to maintain a single schema.

Note; The cases in the two preceding chapters have to some extent been based on real organizations. However, this case is a pure flight of fancy. (The author had been watching too many spy movies when she wrote it!)

Organizational Overview

A group of database designers have been hired to provide updated information systems for the Independent Intelligence Agency (IIA). Given the nature of the agency's work, the designers realize that they will, in some cases, be working with limited information about the way in which the organization functions. In particular, the design team must accept specifications in whatever format they are provided; team members are not permitted to identify or question agency personnel other than the Vice President for Information Services, who has been their sole contact with the organzation. In addition, they will be given few details about the application programs that will be interacting with the database they design.

The Independent Intelligence Agency, headquartered in Geneva, is a nonaligned, worldwide organization that specializes in the gathering and dissemination of covert intelligence. Established during the aftermath of World War II (1947), the IIA is quick to emphasize that while it employs undercover field agents and uses other methods common to intelligence agencies, it has not, is not, and will not be involved in manipulating or in any way influencing the affairs of any country; its sole purpose is to gather information and to sell it to whoever is willing to pay. The IIA will accept commissions to gather specific intelligence as long as doing so does not violate the restriction on becoming active in the affairs of governments. All of IIA's financial resources come from fees paid by clients for information and from investments made with those fees. All transactions are strictly confidential; unauthorized disclosure of information by any employee is cause for immediate dismissal.

The IIA's headquarters building in Geneva contains offices for the Executive Director, Internal Affairs (responsible for monitoring the conduct of field agents, readers, and administrative personnel), Human Resources, and Finance. Because space in the headquarters building is limited, Information Systems has been moved to a renovated warehouse behind the headquarters.

IIA's organization divides the planet into six bureaus, one for each continent except Antarctica. (Any intelligence that comes out of the research stations in Antarctica is handled through one of the northern Canadian stations.) Within the bureaus there are separate *stations* that conduct field operations. Each bureau has a Director, and each station has a Chief who reports to his or her bureau Director. (Note that the central offices for the European Bureau and the Geneva station are on the other side of the city. This arrangement was created to give the Director of the European Bureau and the Chief of the Geneva station the freedom to operate without the constant surveillance of top-level management.)

Stations have three types of people with whom they interact:

- ◆ *Field agents* are actively involved in the collection of intelligence. They are typically full-time employees of the IIA.
- ◆ *Readers* work inside station buildings reviewing print, audio, video, and electronic materials. Much of a reader's work involves intercepting and decoding international cable and satellite transmissions. Readers are typically full-time employees of the IIA.
- ◆ *Informants* are people who are contacted by field agents for information. Informants are usually paid based on the perceived value of the information they provide. They are not IIA employees. Some informants have become so valuable to the IIA, however, that they have been hired as field agents.

Occasionally field agents and readers will exchange roles. For example, a field agent who has spent too long in the field may become a reader and work at that job until retirement. By the same token, a promising reader may undergo field agent training and move into that role.

Stations also have administrative personnel. Although many administrative personnel have little contact with intelligence data or client lists, the security requirements for those employees are as rigorous as for field agents and readers.

Each station has its own budget and manages its own accounting. The Finance Department works at the top organizational level to determine the budget, but once funds are allocated, each station handles the ordering of its own supplies, pays its own expenses (including payments to informants), and cuts its own paychecks. Sales of information may be handled by any level in the organizational hierarchy. Payment is received by the agency making the sale, but all funds are deposited in a single, centralized account in Geneva. The Finance Department's auditors and Internal Affairs staff keep close watch to ensure that all funds collected end up in the bank.

Current Information Systems

IIA maintains a distributed file processing system using ISAM file organization that has been in place since 1974. Each station has its own minicomputer or server that is used to handle the station's accounting functions. These data are available to the Finance Department at the Geneva headquarters building, the station's bureau, and the station's area. Personnel files are kept on the Geneva headquarters' mainframe. The data are available to all stations.

The personnel files, however, contain data about IIA employees only. Each field agent keeps his or her own list of informants. In some cases, those lists have been placed on station computers, but the use is not consistent and in many cases, agents have been reluctant to share their sources.

Data gathered by field agents are stored in the file processing system. The files containing these raw facts are then indexed to allow retrieval by major topics—countries, individuals, and events. An online query language is available, but attempts to retrieve by a characteristic on which there is no index are unacceptably slow.

The IIA does not sell raw facts, but instead sells verified pieces of intelligence. To obtain a sellable piece of intelligence, the IIA must receive confirmation of the same raw fact from several sources. When a field agent or reader reports raw data, he or she also reports a confidence level (from 0 to 100) in the accuracy of that data. Printouts of sorted raw data along with their confidence levels are then examined by readers to find data that support each other with increasing confidence levels. When the confidence levels reach a specific point—IIA will not reveal exactly what that level is—a sellable piece of intelligence is entered into the data file containing sellable merchandise. The reader certifying the piece of intelligence affixes an approximate price, but the exact selling price will be negotiated when the intelligence is actually sold. Of all the tasks that the IIA undertakes, this is the most labor-intensive and delays in certifying sellable intelligence can cost the IIA a significant amount in sales.

The IIA has informed the database designers working on a new information system that application programmers will be preparing an expert system to automate the verification of raw data into sellable pieces of intelligence. Although the database designers will not be given any details on how the expert system will work, they will be told exactly what data the expert system will need to function.

The file processing system has become difficult to maintain. The volume of data added to the files is so high that the station IS staff must reblock the files as often as once every two weeks. The reblocking is time consuming and results in unacceptable downtime during working hours.

Security Concerns

Many of IIA's clients are extremely sensitive to the exclusiveness of the data they are buying: They wish to be the *only* purchasers. Exclusive sales command much higher fees than those for pieces of intelligence that can be sold to more than one buyer.

Some data are also extremely sensitive. The IIA believes that the release of those data to the public would violate the IIA's policy against manipulating or influencing existing governments. Therefore, the security of the intelligence data is of primary concern to the IIA.

The ISAM file system they are currently using has no built-in security. Instead, each record of data added to the files contains a field with a security classification. Each user name that the computer recognizes has a security classification as well. Access to data is granted if the user has a classification equal to or above the classification of the data. The classification scheme is an all-or-nothing affair. Anyone who can supply a user name and password that the computer will recognize receives the classification level of the user name and can read all data at that level or below and can modify all data at that classification level. Since users can modify only data at their classification level, highly privileged users who need to modify data at lower classification levels will have more than one account on the system, once for each classification level below them.

The need for a single user to maintain more than one account has led to numerous security breaches. Users who could not remember all of the user names, passwords, and their associated classification levels have written the information down and either taped it to their monitors in full view of an entire office or placed it in the top center drawer of a desk that is never locked. IIA would therefore like a security system where access can be more tightly tailored to an individual's needs so that only a single account is needed for each user.

The IIA's VP for Information Services has told the design team that the IIA is willing to install retina scanners for user identification in all locations. Portable scanners are also available to be issued with laptop computers.

Equipment Development

To augment its intelligence collection activities, the IIA develops and manufactures about half of its own intelligence gathering equipment. Some of this equipment is then sold to intelligence agencies around the world. In keeping with its position of strict neutrality, the IIA sells equipment to any government that has the money to purchase it.

Currently, control over equipment inventory, usage, testing, and sales is very lax. The VP for Information Services, however, has informed the database design team that a new system must include equipment tracking. Although the equipment development is managed separately from the intelligence gathering, most field equipment tests are performed by field agents and most equipment sales are to clients who also purchase intelligence.

Subject Classifications

The current indexing of the existing data files by commonly used keywords has given the IIA's IS staff an idea that could potentially increase sales of pieces of intelligence. The staff would like to assign subject classifications to verified sellable merchandise, much in the same way a library assigns subject headings to books.

Classifications would then be matched with customers in three ways:

- Subject areas about which a customer wants to be notified whenever something is available.
- Subject areas from which the customer has previously made a purchase.
- Subject areas about which a customer has made a request but then subsequently declined to purchase.

Searches on these matchings of customers and subject classifications could potentially tailor sales calls to client purchasing habits, providing a better use of administrative personnel time.

Summary of IS Needs

The IIA is therefore faced with four major IS problems:

- The file processing system is slow and hard to maintain.
- The file processing system does not provide enough flexibility for current application program technologies. In

particular, it cannot support the expert system that will be created to verify sellable pieces of intelligence.

♦ The system is far less secure than IIA requires.

♦ The distributed file system has led to inconsistencies in the types of data that are stored on the organization's various computers.

To remedy these problems, the IIA has hired a number of IS teams that will be working independently on various parts of the organization's new system. (The isolation of the teams is for security purposes.) The database will still be distributed, but because it will be a true database rather than a file processing system, it will be possible to use a common schema throughout the entire organization.

Accounting functions, which are of interest only to each local station and its supervising bureau, will continue to use the file processing system, at least temporarily. Any upgrades to that system will take place as a separate project.

System Specifications

Prior to hiring the database design team, the bureau directors, continent directors, and local station chiefs came together to prepare a document that described the data they needed in a database. Input for the meeting came from discussions at the stations with field agents, readers, and administrative personnel.

The following outline of data dealing with intelligence gathering and sales that should be stored in the IIA's database was presented to the database design team:

♦ Personnel
- Classification (field agent, reader, or administrative)
- Real name
- Birthdate
- Local country identification number (for example, U.S. social security number)

- Driver's license country (and state, if applicable) and number
- Photo
- Fingerprints
- Retina print
- Height in centimeters
- Weight in kilograms
- Eye color
- Vision
- Current address and phone number
- Aliases (all aliases used, currently or in the past)
  § Name
  § Photo
  § Birthdate
  § Local country identification number (for example, U.S. social security number)
  § Driver's license country (and state, if applicable) and number
  § Height
  § Weight
  § Eye color
  § Address and phone number (if any)
  § Date last used
- All previous addresses including dates of residence
- Family members (parents; all spouses; biological, adopted, step, and foster children; biological, adopted, step, and foster siblings)
  § Real name
  § Birthdate
  § Current address and phone number
  § Highest level of education
  § Current job
  § Photo
- Education (all schools attended and degrees earned)
- Work history
- Criminal record
- Religion
- Organizations other than IIA to which person belongs

- ◆ Informants
  - Real name
  - Birthdate
  - Local country identification number (for example, U.S. social security number)
  - Driver's license country (and state, if applicable) and number
  - Photo
  - Fingerprints
  - Height
  - Weight
  - Eye Color
  - Vision
  - Current address and phone number
  - Aliases (all aliases used, currently or in the past)
    - § Name
    - § Photo
    - § Birthdate
    - § Local country identification number (for example, U.S. social security number)
    - § Driver's license country (and state, if applicable) and number
    - § Height
    - § Weight
    - § Eye color
    - § Address and phone number (if any)
    - § Date last used
  - All previous addresses including dates of residence
  - Family members (parents; all spouses; biological, adopted, step, and foster children; biological, adopted, step, and foster siblings)
    - § Real name
    - § Birthdate
    - § Current address and phone number
    - § Highest level of education
    - § Current job
    - § Photo
  - Education (all schools attended and degrees earned)
  - Work history

- Criminal record
- Religion
- Organizations to which person belongs
- Field agent who recruited the informant
- Contacts made with agents
  - § Date of contact
  - § Outcome of contact
  - § Payment received at contact
  - § Data presented at contact
  - § Agent making the contact

◆ Intelligence data (raw facts)
  - Date collected
  - Source (for example, informant, printed document, agent observation)
  - Location collected (country, city or town)
  - How gathered
  - The data itself
  - Confidence level
  - Cost of the data

◆ Verified piece of intelligence
  - The piece of intelliegence itself
  - Subject classifications
  - Customers who purchased the piece of intelligence
  - Price paid by each customer
  - Date each purchase was made
  - Whether sold exclusively

◆ Customers
  - Name
  - Contact person
  - Address
  - Phone number
  - Fax number
  - Subject classifications of previous purchases
  - Subject classification of previous inquiries that did not lead to purchases

- Subject classifications for which the customer has requested notification
- Purchases made
- Whether customer requires exclusive sales

Internal Affairs, the department responsible, among other things, for monitoring security, wants additional data kept about access to the database:

♦ System logon data (kept about each attempt to log on to the system)
- User ID
- Date
- Time on
- Workstation ID (if access was not from an IIA workstation, but over a phone line, then the phone number from which the call was placed)
- Time off (will be null if logon attempt is unsuccessful)

♦ Information request data
- User ID
- Date
- Time
- Workstation ID or phone number of remote call
- Data item requested
   § Table name
   § Row identifier(s)
- Result (access granted or denied)
- Action performed (retrieve, insert, modify, delete)

The final portion of the database will handle the equipment inventory, testing, use, and sales:

♦ Current equipment inventory
- Classification (for example, tape recorder, microphone, camera)
- Description
- Location (station at which equipment is stored when not in use)

- Current condition
- Restrictions on use

♦ Equipment use records
  - Classification
  - Date used
  - Agent using equipment
  - Where used
  - How used
  - Result of use

♦ Equipment sales
  - Customer
  - Date of purchase
  - Items purchased
  - Amount paid for each item
  - Total amount of purchase

♦ Equipment under development
  - Classification
  - Description
  - Intended use
  - Station where development is taking place
  - Employees involved in development
  - Estimated date of completion
  - Testing data
    § Date of test
    § Type of test
    § Test results
    § Location of test
    § Agent performing test

Designing the Database

One of the drawbacks to the way in which the specifications for the IIA's database have been presented is that they initially appear to be quite well prepared. Each top-level heading seems to correspond to an entity. However, a closer examination of the specifications indicates that each grouping of required data includes multiple entities and often a number of repeating groups.

Probably the easiest way to approach a database design where the specifications are presented in this way is to begin to create an ER diagram. When the database is as large as this one appears to be, it is also easier to break the design into several components (people, intelligence gathering and sales, system security, and equipment tracking).

ER Diagram for People

When looking at the data that are to be stored about people, a database designer is immediately faced with a major decision before drawing a single entity: Should there be separate entities for IIA employees and informants, or should they be a single entity?

When faced with a choice of this type, you need to look carefully at the data that describe the entities. Will the database store the same data about employees as it will about informants? If so, then you are probably dealing with a single entity.

> *Note: An exception to the rule of "same attributes, same entity" occurs when the two entities have different meanings. For example, in an accounting database you may have line item entities for purchase orders that you place to your suppliers and orders that your customers place with you. Although the two entities have exactly the same attributes, their meaning and use are very different and they should be kept as separate entities.*

With the exception of the agent that recruited an informant, the data describing employees and informants is identical. Add to this the fact that informants sometimes become agents and it becomes clear that it makes sense to represent all people as a single entity.

What about that extra attribute that belongs to the informants? (The agent that recruited the informant.) There are two ways to handle it. One is to include it as an attribute of the single person entity. Its value will simply be null for employees. The cost of this solution is the disk space wasted by the large number of nulls. The alternative is to create a separate entity that has a one-to-one relationship with the person entity and contains the person identifier and the agent recruiting the informant. Obtaining the recuiting agent would then require a join between the person entity and the entity holding the extra data. Given that disk space is relatively inexpensive and processor time is very dear, the better choice is to add the attribute to the person entity and allow it to be null where necessary.

Assuming that the design uses one entity for people (named "person"), the portion of the ER diagram that contains data describing people can be found in Figure 11-1. There are eight entities that represent repeating groups of data:

- Fingerprint: Each instance of the Fingerprint entity represents one finger on one hand. Of all the repeating groups, fingerprints are the only ones for which we can make a reasonable estimate of how many there will be. An alternative to including this entity therefore is to use 10 attributes in the Person entity (one for each finger). However, there is no way to guarantee that the IIA has exactly 10 prints for each peson. There may be fewer … or there may be more! (Some people are born with six fingers.) In addition, searching fingerprints would be very clumsy if there were separate attributes for each finger because an application program would need to contain logic to search each individual attribute. However, the current design, which places the repeating group in its own entity, has all fingers in a single attribute. The database stores one instance for each print, regardless of how many there are, and a search routine needs to worry about only one attribute.
- Former Address: Each instance of the Former Address entity represents one place a person has lived. Under the assumption that a person has only one primary residence at any given time, the addresses are distinguished by the date the person moved into the location.

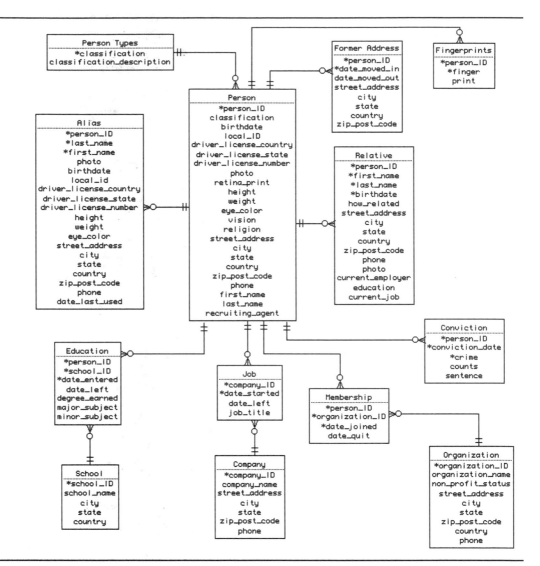

Figure 11-1: Entities required to represent data about people in the IIA database

♦ Relative: There is one instance of the Relative entity for each person that is related to an IIA employee. Choosing a unique identifier for this entity can be a bit tricky. However, it seems reasonable to assume that no one has two relatives with exactly the same name born on the same day.

- ♦ Conviction: Each instance of the Conviction entity represents a conviction for a specific crime on a specific date.
- ♦ Membership: Each instance of the Membership entity represents joining a given organization on a given date. By distinguishing memberships by date, the database can track multiple members in the same organization over time.
- ♦ Job: Each instance of the Job entity represents one job the person has held. The entity identifier is based on the assumption that a person starts only one job with a given company on one day. This entity takes care of a person's job history both at the IIA and prior to joining the IIA. A person's current job will have a date_left value of null.
- ♦ Education: There is one instance of the Education entity for each time a person enrolls in a school. By including the date entered in the entity identifier, the entity can track people who attend a school, take a break, and then return to same school.
- ♦ Alias: Each instance of the alias entity represents one entity used by a person. The entity identifier is based on the assumption that no person has more than one alias with the same name.

ER Diagram for Intelligence Gathering and Sales

The ER diagram that supports intelligence gathering and sales can be found in Figure 11-2. There are three aspects of this diagram that are of particular interest.

First, consider what appear to be the two identical relationships between the Person and Contact entities. If we were to label those relationships, one would represent the agent involved in a contact; the other would represent the informant. As you can see in the Contact entity, there are actually two foreign keys—informant_ID and agent_ID—both of which reference the person_ID in the Person entity. However, the integrity constraint for the foreign key checking is a bit more complicated than simply verifying that a person_ID exists in the Person entity.

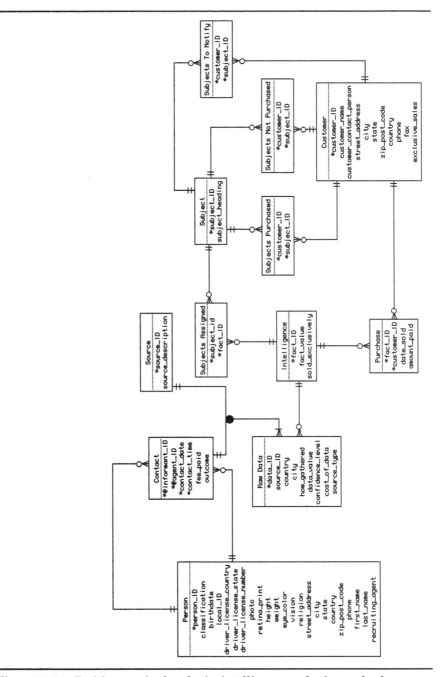

Figure 11-2:   Entities required to depict intelligence gathering and sales

An informant_ID must not only match a person_ID, but the classification of that person must be "informant." By the same token, an agent_ID must have a classification of "agent" as well as matching a person_ID. This is the only way to represent a relationship between two entities of the same type in a relational database. Although other data models may allow circular relationships such as that in Figure 11-3, the relational data model cannot support it because it is a many-to-many relationship. The Contact entity therefore is a composite entity that resolves the relationship between multiple person entities.

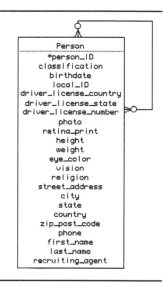

Person
*person_ID
classification
birthdate
local_ID
driver_license_country
driver_license_state
driver_license_number
photo
retina_print
height
weight
eye_color
vision
religion
street_address
city
state
country
zip_post_code
phone
first_name
last_name
recruiting_agent

Figure 11-3:   A circular relationship

The drawback to this approach is a practical one: Most CASE tools are not capable of recognizing primary key–foreign key relationships when the attributes involved do not have the same name. Nor can it automatically recognize the need to verify the classification of a person along with the person's ID. A database designer will therefore need to add a CHECK clause for each column that performs this unusual referential integrity verification.

The second unusual facet of this ER diagram is a type of relationship that you have not seen before: a *mutually exclusive relationship*.

A piece of raw data can come from an informant (the result of a contact) or it can come from another type of source (print, video, electronic, and so on), but it cannot come from both. Therefore, if an instance of the Raw Data entity is related to an instance of the Source entity, it cannot be related to an instance of the Contact entity, and vice versa. We represent this in an ER diagram with a solid black circle between the entities that mutually exclude one another. In this particular case, the relationship can be read: "A piece of raw data comes from one and only one contact or a piece of raw data comes from one and only one source, but not both."

To handle the constraint on the source_ID entity, a database designer must place a CHECK constraint on the entire table created from the entity. (You will see this and other CHECK constraints in the last section of this chapter as part of the discussion of the SQL needed to create this database.) Although source_ID appears to a CASE tool as a foreign key referencing the entity identifier of the Source table, a normal foreign key constraint will not include the possibility that the value is an information ID rather than a source ID.

The third interesting aspect of this ERD is the three relationships between the Subject entity and the Customer entity. As discussed earlier, each of these many-to-many relationships has a different meaning, so although the attributes belonging to each of the three composite entities are identical, they represent completely different things. This is another example of an exception to the rule that if two entities have the same attributes, they are probably the same entity.

ER Diagram for System Security

The ER diagram for the portion of the database that handles system security can be found in Figure 11-4. This diagrams contains one mutually exclusive relationship: the relationship between a data access and raw data or intelligence. A person can access either a piece of raw data or a piece of verified intelligence, but not both in the same access. The remaining relationships between entities are all simple one-to-many relationships.

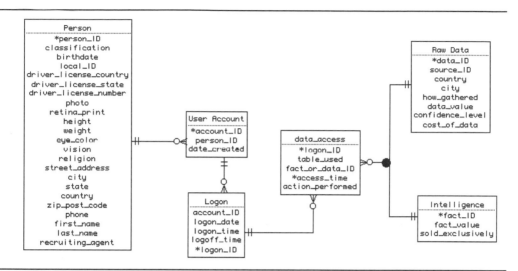

Figure 11-4:   Entities needed to depict system access data

ER Diagram for Equipment Tracking

Equipment tracking (use, development, and sales) requires a fairly straightforward group of entities and relationships (see Figure 11-5). Notice that each piece of equipment is first classified by general type (for example, tape recorder or microphone). It is then given a unique ID so its use can be tracked.

Sale data do not require the individual identifiers of items being sold but only how many of each given type were included. It is therefore up to an application program to delete items sold from inventory. This means that each time an item is sold, an instance of the Equipment Item entity must be deleted. It will therefore be up to the individual who is preparing a shipment of items sold to enter the item identifiers of those items.

The Equipment Item and Under Development Item entities have the same primary key. Should they be combined into one entity? In this case, probably not. Notice that other than the primary key, the entities have no attributes in common. This alone suggests that we are dealing with two different entities. Adding to that the fact that

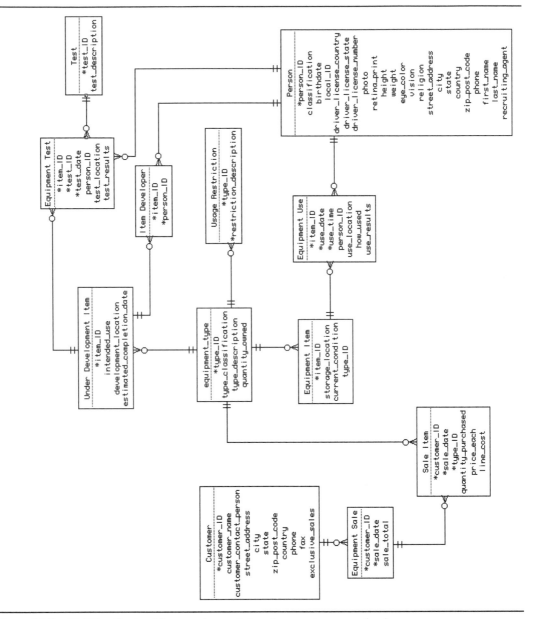

Figure 11-5:   Entities for tracking equipment development, use, and sales

the IIA does not want to retain testing data once a piece of equipment has been certified as ready for everyday use, it is clear that the two entities are indeed distinct.

Designing the Tables

The ER diagrams you have seen translate into the following 33 tables:

```
person (person ID, classification, first_name, last_name, birthdate,
    local_ID, driver_license_country, driver_license_state,
    driver_license_number, photo, retina_print, height, weight,
    eye_color, vision, religion, street_address, city, state,
    country, zip_post_code, phone, recruiting_agent)
person_types (classification, classification_description)
alias (person ID, last name, first name, photo, birthdate, local_ID,
    driver_license_country, driver_license_state,
    driver_license_number, height, weight, eye_color,
    streeet_address, city, state, country, zip_post_code, phone,
    date_last_used)
former_address (person ID, date moved in, date_moved_out,
    street_address, city, state, country, zip_post_code)
education (person ID, school ID, date entered, date_left,
    degree_earned, major_subject, minor_subject)
relative (person ID, first name, last name, birthdate, how_related,
    street_address, city, state, country, zip_post_code, phone,
    photo, current_employer, education, current_job)
school (school ID, school_name, city, state, country)
job (person ID, company ID, date started, date_left, job_title)
company (company ID, company_name, street_address, city, state,
    zip_post_code, phone)
conviction (person ID, conviction date, crime, counts, sentence)
organization (organization ID, organization_name,
    non_profit_status, street_address, city, state, zip_post_code,
    country, phone)
membership (person ID, organization ID, date joined, date_quit)
fingerprints (person ID, finger, print)
contact (informant ID, agent ID, contact date, contact time,
    fee_paid, outcome)
raw_data (data ID, source_ID, source_type, country, city,
    how_gathered, data_value, confidence_level, fact_ID)
source (source ID, source_description)
intelligence (fact ID, fact_value, sold_exclusively)
subject (subject ID, subject_heading)
subjects_assigned (subjectID, fact ID)
customer (customer ID, customer_name, customer_contact_person,
    street_address, city, state, zip_post_code, country, phone, fax,
    exclusive_sales)
```

```
purchase (fact_ID, customer_ID, date_sold, amount_paid)
subjects_purchased (customer_ID, subject_ID)
subjects_not_purchased (customer_ID, subject_ID)
subjects_to_notify (customer_ID, subject_ID)
user_account (account_ID, person_ID, date_created)
logon (logon_ID, account_ID, logon_date, logon_time, logoff_time)
data_access (logon_ID, access_time, table_used, fact_or_data_ID,
    action_performed)
equipment_item (item_ID, storage_location, current_condition,
    type_ID)
usage_restriction (type_ID, restriction_description)
equipment_use (item_ID, use_date, use_time, person_ID, use_location,
    how_used, use_results)
equipment_type (type_ID, type_classification, type_description,
    quantity_owned)
equipment_sale (customer_ID, sale_date, sale_total)
sale_item (customer_ID, sale_date, type_ID, quantity_purchased,
    price_each, line_cost)
```

Because of the circular and mutually exclusive relationships, this set of tables does not document itself as well as other designs, even with its meaningful column and table names. To be understandable, this design definitely needs to be accompanied by a data dictionary that contains explanations for the unusual relationships.

Generating the SQL

The SQL CREATE statements used to install the IIA database appear in Figure 11-6. They contain two elements with which you may not be familiar: BLOBS and CHECK constraints.

BLOBS

Unlike the databases discussed previously in this book, the IIA database contains images. DBMSs use two general strategies for storing images. The first is to link image files to the database by storing a path name to a separate image file. The second is to actually store the images as part of the database itself, usually in a column with a data type of BLOB (binary large object).

The first strategy keeps the database smaller, but you run the risk of not being able to access an image if the image file is moved or deleted. By keeping the image within the database, you can be assured

```
CREATE TABLE person
(
    person_ID INT,
    classification INT,
    birthdate DATE,
    local_ID CHAR (15),
    driver_license_country CHAR (15),
    driver_license_state CHAR (15),
    driver_license_number CHAR (15),
    photo BLOB,
    retina_print BLOB,
    height DECIMAL (5,1),
    weight DECIMAL (5,1),
    eye_color CHAR (10),
    vision CHAR (10),
    religion CHAR (15),
    street_address CHAR (30),
    city CHAR (30),
    state CHAR (30),
    country CHAR (30),
    zip_post_code CHAR (10),
    phone CHAR (15),
    first_name CHAR (15),
    last_name CHAR (15),
    recruiting_agent INT,
    PRIMARY KEY (person_ID),
    FOREIGN KEY (classification) REFERENCES person_types
);

CREATE TABLE person_types
(
    classification INT,
    classification_description CHAR (15),
    PRIMARY KEY (classification)
);

CREATE TABLE former_address
(
    person_ID INT,
    date_moved_in DATE,
    date_moved_out DATE,
    street_address CHAR (30),
    city CHAR (30),
    state CHAR (30),
    country CHAR (30),
    zip_post_code CHAR (10),
    PRIMARY KEY (person_ID, date_moved_in),
    FOREIGN KEY (person_ID) REFERENCES person
);
```

Figure 11-6 :   SQL statements to create the IIA database

```
CREATE TABLE alias
(
    person_ID INT,
    last_name CHAR (15),
    first_name CHAR (15),
    photo BLOB,
    birthdate DATE,
    local_id CHAR (15),
    driver_license_country CHAR (15),
    driver_license_state CHAR (15),
    driver_license_number CHAR (15),
    height DECIMAL (5,1),
    weight DECIMAL (5,1),
    eye_color CHAR (10),
    street_address CHAR (30),
    city CHAR (30),
    state CHAR (30),
    country CHAR (30),
    zip_post_code CHAR (10),
    phone CHAR (15),
    date_last_used DATE,
    PRIMARY KEY (person_ID, last_name, first_name),
    FOREIGN KEY (person_ID) REFERENCES person
);

CREATE TABLE relative
(
    person_ID INT,
    first_name CHAR (15),
    last_name CHAR (15),
    birthdate DATE,
    how_related CHAR (30),
    street_address CHAR (30),
    city CHAR (30),
    state CHAR (30),
    country CHAR (30),
    zip_post_code CHAR (10),
    phone CHAR (15),
    photo BLOB,
    current_employer CHAR (30),
    education CHAR (30),
    current_job CHAR (30),
    PRIMARY KEY (person_ID, first_name, last_name, birthdate),
    FOREIGN KEY (person_ID) REFERENCES person
);
```

Figure 11-6 (Continued):   SQL statements to create the IIA database

```
CREATE TABLE education
(
    person_ID INT,
    school_ID INT,
    date_entered DATE,
    date_left DATE,
    degree_earned CHAR (10),
    major_subject CHAR (15),
    minor_subject CHAR (15),
    PRIMARY KEY (person_ID, school_ID, date_entered) );

CREATE TABLE school
(
    school_ID INT,
    school_name CHAR (50),
    city CHAR (30),
    state CHAR (30),
    country CHAR (30),
    PRIMARY KEY (school_ID) );

CREATE TABLE job
(
    company_ID INT,
    date_started DATE,
    date_left DATE,
    job_title CHAR (50),
    person_ID INT,
    PRIMARY KEY (company_ID, date_started),
    FOREIGN KEY (company_ID) REFERENCES company,
    FOREIGN KEY (person_ID) REFERENCES person );

CREATE TABLE company
(
    company_ID INT,
    company_name CHAR (50),
    street_address CHAR (30),
    city CHAR (30),
    state CHAR (30),
    zip_post_code CHAR (10),
    phone CHAR (15),
    PRIMARY KEY (company_ID) );

CREATE TABLE fingerprints
(
    person_ID INT,
    finger CHAR (15),
    print BLOB,
    PRIMARY KEY (person_ID, finger),
    FOREIGN KEY (person_ID) REFERENCES person );
```

Figure 11-6 (Continued):   SQL statements to create the IIA database

```
CREATE TABLE conviction
(
    person_ID INT,
    conviction_date DATE,
    crime CHAR (50),
    counts INT,
    sentence CHAR (50),
    PRIMARY KEY (person_ID, conviction_date, crime) );

CREATE TABLE organization
(
    organization_ID INT,
    organization_name CHAR (50),
    non_profit_status CHAR (1),
    street_address CHAR (30),
    city CHAR (30),
    state CHAR (30),
    zip_post_code CHAR (10),
    country CHAR (30),
    phone CHAR (15),
    PRIMARY KEY (organization_ID) );

CREATE TABLE membership
(
    person_ID INT,
    organization_ID INT,
    date_joined DATE,
    date_quit DATE,
    PRIMARY KEY (person_ID, organization_ID, date_joined),
    FOREIGN KEY (person_ID) REFERENCES person,
    FOREIGN KEY (organization_ID) REFERENCES organization );

CREATE TABLE contact
(
    informant_ID INT
        CHECK (EXISTS (SELECT * FROM person
            WHERE VALUE = person_ID and classification = 4)),
    agent_ID INT
        CHECK (EXISTS (SELECT * FROM person
            WHERE VALUE = person_ID and classification = 1)),
    contact_date DATE,
    contact_time TIME,
    fee_paid DECIMAL (8,2),
    outcome CHAR (50),
    PRIMARY KEY (informant_ID, agent_ID, contact_date,
        contact_time));
```

Figure 11-6 (Continued):   **SQL statements to create the IIA database**

```
CREATE TABLE raw_data
(
    data_ID INT,
    source_ID INT,
    source_type CHAR (!5),
    country CHAR (30),
    city CHAR (30),
    how_gathered CHAR (50),
    data_value CHAR (255),
    confidence_level INT,
    cost_of_data DECIMAL (8,2),
    fact_ID INT,
    PRIMARY KEY (data_ID),
    FOREIGN KEY (fact_ID) REFERENCES intelligence
    CHECK (source_type = 'informant' AND
        EXISTS (SELECT * FROM person
        WHERE source_ID = person_ID AND classification = 4)
        OR
        source_type = 'document' AND
        EXISTS (SELECT * FROM source
        WHERE source_ID = source.source_ID)));

CREATE TABLE source
(
    source_ID INT,
    source_description CHAR (255),
    PRIMARY KEY (source_ID) );

CREATE TABLE intelligence
(
    fact_ID INT,
    fact_value CHAR (255),
    sold_exclusively CHAR (1),
    PRIMARY KEY (fact_ID) );

CREATE TABLE subject
(
    subject_ID INT,
    subject_heading CHAR (50),
    PRIMARY KEY (subject_ID) );

CREATE TABLE subjects_assigned
(
    subject_ID INT,
    fact_ID INT,
    PRIMARY KEY (subject_ID, fact_ID),
    FOREIGN KEY (subject_ID) REFERENCES subject,
    FOREIGN KEY (fact_ID) REFERENCES intelligence );
```

Figure 11-6 (Continued):   SQL statements to create the IIA database

```
CREATE TABLE customer
(
    customer_ID INT,
    customer_name CHAR (50),
    customer_contact_person CHAR (50),
    street_address CHAR (30),
    city CHAR (30),
    state CHAR (30),
    zip_post_code CHAR (10),
    country CHAR (30),
    phone CHAR (15),
    fax CHAR (15),
    exclusive_sales CHAR (1),
    PRIMARY KEY (customer_ID) );

CREATE TABLE purchase
(
    fact_ID INT,
    customer_ID INT,
    date_sold DATE,
    amount_paid DECIMAL (8,2),
    PRIMARY KEY (fact_ID, customer_ID),
    FOREIGN KEY (fact_ID) REFERENCES intelligence,
    FOREIGN KEY (customer_ID) REFERENCES customer );

CREATE TABLE subjects_purchased
(
    customer_ID INT,
    subject_ID INT,
    PRIMARY KEY (customer_ID, subject_ID),
    FOREIGN KEY (customer_ID) REFERENCES customer,
    FOREIGN KEY (subject_ID) REFERENCES subject );

CREATE TABLE subjects_not_purchased
(
    customer_ID INT,
    subject_ID INT,
    PRIMARY KEY (customer_ID, subject_ID),
    FOREIGN KEY (customer_ID) REFERENCES customer,
    FOREIGN KEY (subject_ID) REFERENCES subject );

CREATE TABLE subjects_to_notify
(
    customer_ID INT,
    subject_ID INT,
    PRIMARY KEY (customer_ID, subject_ID),
    FOREIGN KEY (customer_ID) REFERENCES customer,
    FOREIGN KEY (subject_ID) REFERENCES subject );
```

Figure 11-6 (Continued): SQL statements to create the IIA database

```
CREATE TABLE user_account
(
    account_ID INTCHAR (10),
    person_ID INT,
    date_created DATE,
    PRIMARY KEY (account_ID),
    FOREIGN KEY (person_ID) REFERENCES person
);

CREATE TABLE logon
(
    account_ID INTCHAR (10),
    logon_date DATE,
    logon_time TIME,
    logoff_time TIME,
    logon_ID INT,
    PRIMARY KEY (logon_ID),
    FOREIGN KEY (account_ID) REFERENCES user_account
);

CREATE TABLE data_access
(
    logon_ID INT,
    table_used CHAR (30),
    fact_or_data_ID INT,
    access_time TIME,
    action_performed CHAR (30),
    PRIMARY KEY (logon_ID, access_time),
    FOREIGN KEY (logon_ID) REFERENCES logon
    CHECK (table_used = 'raw_data' AND
        EXISTS (SELECT * FROM raw_date
        WHERE fact_or_data_ID = data_ID)
        OR
        (table_used = 'intelligence' AND
        EXISTS (SELECT * FROM intelligence
        WHERE fact_or_data_ID = fact_ID))
);

CREATE TABLE equipment_item
(
    item_ID INT,
    storage_location CHAR (30),
    current_condition CHAR (10),
    type_ID INT,
    PRIMARY KEY (item_ID),
    FOREIGN KEY (type_ID) REFERENCES equipment_type
);
```

Figure 11-6 (Continued):   SQL statements to create the IIA database

```
CREATE TABLE usage_restriction
(
    type_ID INT,
    restriction_description CHAR (50),
    PRIMARY KEY (type_ID, restriction_description),
    FOREIGN KEY (type_ID) REFERENCES equipment_type );

CREATE TABLE equipment_use
(
    item_ID INT,
    use_date DATE,
    use_time TIME,
    person_ID INT,
    use_location CHAR (50),
    how_used CHAR (255),
    use_results CHAR (255),
    PRIMARY KEY (item_ID, use_date, use_time),
    FOREIGN KEY (item_ID) REFERENCES equipment_item,
    FOREIGN KEY (person_ID) REFERENCES person );

CREATE TABLE equipment_type
(
    type_ID INT,
    type_classification CHAR (15),
    type_description CHAR (50),
    quantity_owned INT,
    PRIMARY KEY (type_ID) );

CREATE TABLE equipment_sale
(
    customer_ID INT,
    sale_date DATE,
    sale_total DECIMAL (8,2),
    PRIMARY KEY (customer_ID, sale_date),
    FOREIGN KEY (customer_ID) REFERENCES customer );

CREATE TABLE sale_item
(
    customer_ID INT,
    sale_date DATE,
    type_ID INT,
    quantity_purchased INT,
    price_each DECIMAL (8,2),
    line_cost DECIMAL (8,2),
    PRIMARY KEY (customer_ID, sale_date, type_ID),
    FOREIGN KEY (customer_ID) REFERENCES equipment_sale,
    FOREIGN KEY (sale_date) REFERENCES equipment_sale,
    FOREIGN KEY (type_ID) REFERENCES equipment_type );
```

Figure 11-6 (Continued):   SQL statements to create the IIA database

```
CREATE TABLE under_development_item
(
    item_ID INT,
    intended_use CHAR (50),
    development_location CHAR (50),
    estimated_completion_date DATE,
    type_ID INT,
    PRIMARY KEY (item_ID),
    FOREIGN KEY (type_ID) REFERENCES equipment_type
);

CREATE TABLE item_developer
(
    item_ID INT,
    person_ID INT,
    PRIMARY KEY (item_ID, person_ID),
    FOREIGN KEY (person_ID) REFERENCES person
);

CREATE TABLE equipment_test
(
    item_ID INT,
    test_ID INT,
    test_date DATE,
    person_ID INT,
    test_location CHAR (50),
    test_results CHAR (255),
    PRIMARY KEY (item_ID, test_ID, test_date),
    FOREIGN KEY (item_ID) REFERENCES under_development_item,
    FOREIGN KEY (test_ID) REFERENCES test,
    FOREIGN KEY (person_ID) REFERENCES person
);

CREATE TABLE test
(
    test_ID INT,
    test_description CHAR (255),
    PRIMARY KEY (test_ID)
);
```

Figure 11-6 (Continued):   SQL statements to create the IIA database

that the image is always available. That is why the columns in the
IIA database that will hold images have a data type of BLOB.

> *Note: You may not have a choice in the way in which you store
> images in a database because often a DBMS will not support
> both image storage strategies.*

CHECK Constraints

The IIA database has three instances of unusual relationships: one circular relationship and two mutually exclusive relationships. To enforce the integrity of those relationships, a database designer must add CHECK constraints to the SQL CREATE statements; standard foreign key constraints will not suffice.

To handle the circular relationship, a database designer adds the CHECK constraints to the columns:

```
informant_ID INT
    CHECK (EXISTS (SELECT * FROM person
        WHERE VALUE = person_ID and classification = 4)),
agent_ID INT
    CHECK (EXISTS (SELECT * FROM person
        WHERE VALUE = person_ID and classification = 1)),
```

The constraint is met if the expression within parentheses is true. Therefore, if some row exists in the Person table that has a value matching the informant_ID and a classification of informant (the code value 4), then the constraint is met. By the same token, if a row exists in the Person table that has a value matching the agent_ID and a classification of agent (the code value 1), then the constraint is met.

To handle the mutually exclusive relationships, each CHECK constraint contains two retrievals linked by an OR. Because the constraints require values from two columns in each table, the constraints are most easily implemented as table constraints:

```
CHECK (source_type = 'informant' AND
    EXISTS (SELECT * FROM person
    WHERE source_ID = person_ID AND classification = 4)
    OR
    source_type = 'document' AND
    EXISTS (SELECT * FROM source
    WHERE source_ID = source.source_ID))

CHECK (table_used = 'raw_data' AND
    EXISTS (SELECT * FROM raw_date
    WHERE fact_or_data_ID = data_ID)
    OR
    (table_used = 'intelligence' AND
    EXISTS (SELECT * FROM intelligence
    WHERE fact_or_data_ID = fact_ID)
```

In both cases, the constraint first determines which type of source or table has been used. It then verifies that a matching row exists in the correct table.

In most cases, it is impossible to enforce mutually exclusive relationships and verify their integrity without including a column in the table that indicates which of the mutually exclusive options has been chosen. This happens because the numeric identifiers assigned to entities are independent and meaningless and do not necessarily represent unique sets of values. Assume, for example, that a row is entered into the Data Access table with a fact_or_data_ID of 1019. As it so happens, this is a piece of raw data. However, there is a fact_ID of 1019 but no data_ID with that value. If the CHECK constraint were written

```
CHECK (EXISTS (SELECT * FROM raw_date
    WHERE fact_or_data_ID = data_ID)
    OR
    EXISTS (SELECT * FROM intelligence
    WHERE fact_or_data_ID = fact_ID)
```

then the constraint would be valid, even though there was no matching raw data ID.

Glossary

Attribute: A property of an entity; data that describe an entity; a column in a relation.

Base table: A table whose data are physically stored in a database.

Case sensitive: Distinguishing between upper- and lowercase letters.

CASE (computer-aided software engineering) tool: A piece of software used to support the design and development of information systems and application software.

Catalog: Another term for a data dictionary.

Clustering: Grouping data together on the same disk page to improve retrieval performance.

Column homogeneous: A property of a relation stating that all the values in a given column are taken from the same domain.

Commit: End a transaction by making its changes permanent.

Composite entity: An entity that represents the relationship between two other entities.

Concatenated identifier: An entity identifier made up of the values of more than one attribute.

Constraint: A rule to which some element in a database must adhere.

Context diagram: The top-level diagram in a data flow diagram that shows the environmental context in which the information system exists.

Data dictionary: A repository for data describing the structural elements of a database.

Data dictionary driven: A property of relational databases in which all access to stored data is preceded by access to the data dictionary to determine if the requested data elements exist and if the user has the access rights to perform the requested action.

Data flow: The path taken by data as they are processed throughout an organization.

Data flow diagram: A diagram that shows the data flows in an organization, including sources of data, where data are stored, and processes that transform data.

Data model: A formal way of describing the relationship between entities in a database to a database management system.

Data store: In a data flow diagram, a place where data are stored.

Database: A place where data are stored along with definitions of the relationships between those data.

Database management system: Software that provides access to the data in a database; translates a user's requests for data that are framed in terms of logical relationships into physical storage access commands.

Deletion anomaly: A problem that occurs in poorly designed relations such that a user accidentally loses data that should be kept when deleting part of a primary key forces removal of an entire row from a relation.

Determinant: An attribute upon which another attribute is functionally dependent.

Domain: An expression of the permissible values for an attribute.

Domain constraint: A rule that requires that all values of an attribute come from a specified domain.

Entity: Anything about which data are stored in a database.

Entity identifier: An attribute or combination of attributes whose values will uniquely identify every instance of an entity.

Entity integrity: A constraint on a relation that states that no part of a primary key may be null.

Entity-relationship diagram: A diagram that shows the relationships between entities in a database environment.

Equi-join: A join based on matching identical values.

Foreign key: A column or combination of columns that is the same as the primary key of a table in the same database.

Functional dependency: A relationship between two attributes such that at any given time, for each unique value of attribute A in the database, there is only one value of attribute B.

Horizontal partitioning: Splitting the rows of a table into multiple table to improve retrieval performance.

Index: An ordered list of key values that provides a fast access path to the data in a relation.

Inner join: An equi-join.

Insertion anomaly: A problem that occurs in poorly designed relations such that a user is prevented from entering data because values for all the columns of a primary key are not available.

Instance (of a relation): A relation that contains rows of data values.

Instance (of an entity): A real-world occurrence of an entity represented by values for the entity's attributes.

Join: An operation from the relational algebra that combines two relations by matching rows based on values in columns in the two tables. The matching relationship is usually primary key to foreign key.

Many-to-many relationship: A relationship between two entities in which an instance of entity A can be related to zero, one, or more instances of entity B and an instance of entity B can be related to zero, one, or more instances of entity A.

Metadata: Data about data; the data stored in a data dictionary.

Modification anomaly: A problem with a poor designed relation that occurs when unnecessary duplicated data are not updated consistently and data that should have identical values do not.

Multivalued: Having the potential to contain more than one value at any given time.

Multivalued dependency: A dependency between three attributes in which attribute A determines a small but finite set of values for attribute B and attribute A also determines a small but finite set of values for attribute C, but attributes B and C are independent.

Mutually exclusive relationship: A relationship in which an instance of entity A can be related to either an instance of entity B or an instance of entity C, but not both.

Natural equi-join: An equi-join.

Normal form: Design criteria that a relation must meet.

Normalization: The process of placing attributes into tables that avoid the problems associated with poor database design.

Null: A special value meaning "unknown."

One-to-many relationship: A relationship between two entities in which an instance of entity A can be related to zero, one, or more instances of entity B and entity B can be related to at most one instance of entity A.

One-to-one relationship: A relationship between two entities in which an instance of entity A can be related to at most one instance of entity B and entity B can be related to at most one instance of entity A.

Page: The size of the block of data that a computer (and therefore a database) transfers between disk and main memory at one time.

Partitioning: Breaking relations into parts to improve retrieval performance.

Physical schema: The physical storage structures used to store the data in a database.

Precision: The number of digits to the right of the decimal point in a number.

Predicate: A logical expression against which data are evaluated.

Primary key: One or more columns whose values uniquely identify every row in a relation.

Process: In a data flow diagram, something that is done to or with data.

Prototyping: A process for system and database design in which users respond to increasingly specific designs of the interface of an application program; useful in cases where system specifications are not thoroughly known in advance.

Query optimizer: That portion of a database management system that selects the most efficient strategy for processing a query.

Referential integrity: A constraint on a relation that states that every nonnull foreign key value must reference an existing primary key value.

Relation: The definition of the structure of a two-dimensional table made up of columns and rows.

Relational database: A database in which the only data structures are relations.

Relationship data: Data that describe the relationship between two entities rather than each of the individual entities.

Repeating group: An attribute that has more than one value in each row of a relation.

Roll back: End a transaction by undoing all its actions so the database is restored to the state it was in when the transaction began.

Schema: The overall logical plan of a database.

Single-valued: Having only a single value at any given time.

Table: A relation in a relational database.

Temporary table: A base table that exists only in main memory and for the length of a given database session.

Three-schema architecture: Three ways of looking at a database through the physical schema, the logical schema, and user views of data.

Three-valued logic: A set of logical truth tables that include the values true, false, and unknown.

Transaction: A unit of work submitted to a database.

Transitive dependency: A group of functional dependencies such that attribute A determines attribute B, which in turn determines attribute C. Therefore, it is also true that attribute A determines attribute C.

Tuple: A row in a relation.

Update anomaly: Another term for a modification anomaly.

Vertical partitioning: Splitting the columns of a table into multiple tables to improve retrieval performance.

View: A named query store in a data dictionary that is used to create a virtual table whenever a user includes the name of the view in a data access request.

Virtual table: A table in a relational database that exists only in main memory.

Weak entity: An entity that cannot exist in a database unless an instance of another entity is present and related to it.

Index